Screenwriting 101
The Essential Craft of Feature Film Writing
Neill D. Hicks

"Straight talk for beginning screenwriters, full of common sense, wit, and good humor. Neill's to-the-point discussion of the logic of screenplay formatting is particularly helpful."

--Beverly Gray, Screenwriting Instructor, UCLA Extension Writers' Program, and Story Editor for Roger Corman's Concorde--New Horizons Pictures

"A sensible, spirited primer on the task of screenwriting by someone who's been there. In a breezy, lucid style, Neill emphasizes the development of craft and the importance of narrative drive in the telling of a screen story."

--Dennis Palumbo, Screenwriter, *My Favorite Year*, "Welcome Back, Kotter", author, and psychotherapist

"Neill's screenwriting classes are among the most popular at UCLA and if you've ever attended one, you know why. His book is every bit as comprehensive, informative and entertaining as his classes."

--Robby London, Screenwriter and Executive Vice President, Creative Affairs, DIC Entertainment

"Neill's book is great. He has managed to boil down the essence of good screenwriting into a few concise chapters. Everyone who wants to work in Hollywood, and NOT just writers, should read this book and take the information to heart."

--Roberta Chow, Co-Producer, *Rumble in the Bronx*

"A must-read for aspiring screenwriters . . . buy this book BEFORE you even turn on your computer!"

--Ben Moses, Producer, *Good Morning, Vietnam*

"Neill delivers a great balance of what new screenwriters WANT to know and what they NEED to know. If you can't attend his class, read this book!"

--Laurel Tokuda, Director, Canadian Television and Film Institute for Screenwriters

"Students of screenwriting at last have available a resource that is practical, accessible, comprehensible and unreservedly informative. Here is a guide with authority. Screenwriting 101 never fails the student, and never dishonors the craft. Buy it, dog-ear it, split the spine to shreds!"

--Pamala Karol, Screenwriting Instructor, Loyola Marymount University

"At last, Neill's insights and power of analysis are available to both the aspiring screenwriter and the seasoned filmmaker who realize that the art of writing is like Tai Chi, a never-ending evolution of self-improvement."

--Brian Trenchard-Smith, Director of 27 films, including *Happy Face Murders* and *Brittanic*

"Screenwriting 101 provides the most thorough and accurate explanation of the work-a-day business world of screenwriting I've ever read. Neill Hicks makes complex writing concepts surprisingly easy to grasp, in a way that only a master teacher can. And he does so while keeping his book one hell of a fun read."

--Eric Edson, Screenwriter, and Executive Director of the Hollywood Symposium

"Smart, witty, literate, wise and rigorous, this is essential reading for the beginning screenwriter. The novice screenwriter should read this book immediately and take its wisdom to heart. The advanced writer should buy it and re-read it every six months to remember what the craft of writing movies is all about."

--Jim Sauvé, Screenwriter, Instructor at UCLA Extension Writers' Program

"Neill articulates what successful screenwriters have instinctively known for decades. If you want to write hit movies, read this book."

--James Bruner and Elizabeth Stevens, Screenwriters, *Missing in Action, Invasion USA, The Delta Force, An Eye for an Eye*

SCREENWRITING 101

THE ESSENTIAL CRAFT OF FEATURE FILM WRITING

BY

NEILL D. HICKS

Published by Michael Wiese Productions, 11288 Ventura Blvd., Suite 821, Studio City, CA 91604, (818) 379-8799 Fax (818) 986-3408.
E-mail: wiese@earthlink.net
http://www.mwp.com

Cover design, by The Art Hotel
Interior design and layout by Gina Mansfield

Printed by McNaughton & Gunn, Inc., Saline, Michigan
Manufactured in the United States of America

Library of Congress Cataloging-in-Publication Data

Hicks, Neill D., 1946 -
    Screenwriting 101: the essential craft of feature film writing/
    by Neill D. Hicks.
       p.   cm.
    ISBN 0-94-118872-8
    1. Motion picture authorship. I. Title. II. Title: Screenwriting
    one hundred one III. Title: Screenwriting one hundred and one
    PN 1996.H48 1999
    808.2'3--dc21
                                                              99-30724
                                                                  CIP

Dedication

E.T.

"There is nothing so good for the inside of a man as the outside of a horse."
— Winston Churchill

SCREENWRITING 101
BY NEILL D. HICKS

TABLE OF CONTENTS

INTRODUCTION

The horror film producer has rejected more than a dozen ideas presented by the screenwriter sitting on the opposite side of his desk, and now he decides he's going to tell the writer what kind of story he wants for a movie. Naturally, when a producer speaks, a screenwriter listens eagerly.

The mogul pauses for a moment, leans back in his chair, watches his cigar smoke stream toward the ceiling, and drifts into the patented, self-absorbed Hollywood producer reverie: Two couples go to spend a weekend in their mountain cabin, where they are promptly snowed in by a surprise blizzard. Trapped without enough food and with no way down the mountain, one of the men decides to brave the elements for help. Unfortunately, that's the last the remaining three people see of him. After another day of going hungry and cold, the second husband resolves to get down the mountain for help. Leaving the two women alone, he staggers off through the snowdrifts into oblivion.

Meanwhile, the two women are getting pretty hungry. In desperation they trap a chicken (*in the blizzard!*) and decide to eat it raw. One of the women with enough nerve slices open the bird — and discovers her husband's severed finger inside!

The proud producer crams the cigar back into his mouth, throws the writer a knowing look, and waits for the inevitable awestruck response. "Uh, well," I have the temerity to ask, "how did the finger get into the chicken?"

Instantly the producer lurches forward, throws himself across the desk, jabs the cigar into my face and yells, "Hell, *I* don't know. *You're* the writer!"

It was my first prophetic Hollywood experience—the screenwriter has to stuff the finger in the chicken. It is the screenwriter's job to make the story *work*.

Of all the people on the moviemaking team, the screenwriter is the only true, originating creative force, the sleight-of-hand artist who makes sense out of a chaotic world for the audience.

This book is about *satisfying* the theatrical feature film audience. It is not the unified theory of film criticism. It is not a fill-in-the-blanks, five-easy-steps to a successful screenplay. There are no formulas, no magical incantations, and no previously unrevealed secrets. Instead, there are techniques for trying out your ideas, devices for approaching the elements of screen drama, and ways of learning to think like a screenwriter.

The book is about screenwriting by a screenwriter, and all of the suggestions offered in these pages come from the perspective of more than twenty years of making my living as a writer, not as a critic or an analyst. Additionally, I have taught screenwriting as a guest instructor at numerous universities and institutes throughout the world, and those experiences have allowed me to investigate how the craft of screenwriting can be communicated to other people.

Naturally, you will be able to find an abundance of exceptions to the advice and examples offered in these pages if you choose to look for them. But exceptions don't invalidate the advice, nor does the advice contained here negate the work of other writers. We simply differ in our approach to the craft. You will ultimately choose how you write as well as what you write about. All this book can do is offer you the best guidance I know of based on my years behind a pencil. None of the techniques I want to share with you are meant to be dogmatic truth—no matter how adamantly I may defend my particular point of view. As Rudyard Kipling said, "There are nine-and-sixty ways of constructing tribal lays, And every single one of them is right." That's the kind of paradox that makes Hollywood interesting as well as crazy-making. Take what's valuable for you right now, and leave the rest for another time. After some years of writing experience, you'll begin to pull the recommendations, admonitions, and instructions together into your own philosophy of what screenwriting is all about.

Keep a pencil in your hand as you read this book. Make notes in the margins. Doodle your reactions and thoughts as you read, right here in the book. In fact, there are *Scribble Exercises* built in every few pages, specific activities and questions to stir your reactions. For the most part, these *Scribble Exercises* call for immediate, intuitive responses, so you will continually go back to erase and revise your notes as you read.

Go ahead, make a mess of it.

It's that kind of book.

All right, grab a pencil, turn the page, and let's see what the screen-writer has to do in order to satisfy the audience.

Chapter One

DRAMA IS CONFLICT

"The plot must be so structured, even without benefit of any visual effect, that the one who is hearing the events unroll shudders with fear and feels pity at what happens."

— Aristotle, *Poetics*

Humankind has told stories for thousands of years. We have squatted around innumerable campfires to hear the tribal yarn spinner weave the magic of words into a fabric of cultural expectation and mythical archives. And somewhere in the development of our nascent entertainment culture we developed a taste for more engaging stories in the form of drama. But, long before Aristotle and Shakespeare refined the dramatic form and codified it into the comedies and tragedies we know today, the earliest forms of drama were probably sporting contests, ritualized combats between two opponents who wrestled against each other for the same goal—the glory of winning.

Two oiled and naked young men face each other in the sandy ring. They are both vigorous and skilled, the best their culture has to offer. They are both worthy; each of them represents the highest values of strength and courage that the society considers to be important. The only unknown is which of these young men will triumph, so the audience roots for one favorite homeboy or the other until the test of strength and skill is complete.

These ancient contests were not very different from the college and professional basketball or football games we watch today. We choose a side in the conflict based on some imagined or generated loyalty such as the city the team claims as home or the unity we feel with our alma mater. But while these sporting contests may be exciting, they are not wholly satisfying because there is no value in question that will force a change for either the participants or the audience. No matter which side wins, our lives are likely to go on in pretty much the same way they did two hours earlier.

Likewise, for our epic wrestlers, equally matched and equally deserving though they may be, the two chums gyrating in the dirt already share *precisely the same values*. Simply by entering into the match, each of the contestants has exhibited the values of the culture—youth, strength, courage, skill—and no matter which of them wins the battle, they will probably go out after the match to knock back a few ambrosias together and share their consolidated glory. And while the individual audience members may have cheered for their neighborhood favorite, or even had a drachma or two wagered on the side, the fact is that nothing has been gained or lost in the contest beyond bragging rights. There is no *moral valence* attached to winning or losing.

Imagine, however, there is a *good* guy and a *bad* guy who are wrestling. Each of the contestants represents a system of values. One system we'll call *good*, because we in the audience share those values; and one system we'll call *bad*, because it is a set of rules and behaviors that we do not agree with and that cannot coexist with our system of rules and behaviors. If the wrestlers are fighting in our stead, that is, if we will be bound by the result of the fight, then our lives will be irrevocably changed by the outcome. If the bad guy wins, our lives will be adversely transformed. If the good guy wins, our lives will be enhanced. In these circumstances we are far more invested in the *change* that will result as a consequence of the battle. Something is at stake in our lives. Now we have *drama.*

Drama is conflict. It is about somebody who acts against somebody else. Yet, it is more than mere opposition because drama is about conflict that results in a *significant transition* in the lives of the participants—it alters both the characters and their surrounding society.

2

DRAMA MAKES SENSE

But drama is more than just a list of events where *this happens and then that happens and then something else happens.* Drama tells a *story,* a *this happens and because of it, that happens.* Drama provides a cause-and-effect structure that gives us a paradigm for making sense of life.

Drama is not life. Life is ordinary. You get up in the morning, brush your teeth, eat breakfast, go to work, have a flat tire, take the dog to the vet, etc. The events of daily life are a catalogue of occurrences that are largely without clear, satisfying resolution. There may be highs and lows, sensational moments, excitement and disappointment, but for the most part, life is an episodic roster of everyday affairs which have more or less equal significance.

Drama, however, is encapsulated life, life condensed to its essences and raised to its heights. It is a linear, narrative arrangement of events in which someone acts against someone else—conflict—and in which every event in that sequence directly impacts the success or failure of a noteworthy life transition. *Rocky* isn't about the history of boxing, but the change one man makes as he finds the strength to pursue a dream. *Ordinary People* is about Conrad's change in the relationship with his mother, and the consequences of that change on his family. *Rain Man* is the story of Charlie Babbitt's change in the way he relates to other people brought on by his relationship with one person, his autistic savant brother, Raymond. *Braveheart* is about the change in a much larger society brought about by one man's transition from complacent submission to defiant resistance.

Let's say then that

Ordered

Drama is ^ Conflict

3

The screenwriter's job is to extract the consequential incidents from life and arrange them in an emphatic sequence to tell the *story* of the transition. To do this, the screenwriter compresses time and collapses events.

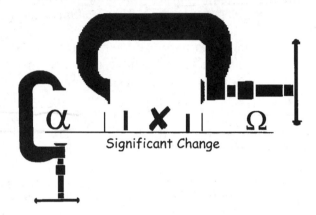

Significant Change

The imaginative screenwriter has available all time and all space from which to draw a story. For the sake of convenience, we can represent this availability of material as a simple continuum, the Alpha to Omega of existence, from the Big Bang to the Big Squeeze. Obviously, the entire history of the universe is too much material to write a screenplay about, so the screenwriter begins to compress time into a manageable proportion.

Whether the time selected for the story is present day, a thousand years in the past, or a hundred years in the future, the screenwriter has limited the scope of the story. Depending on the particular story, the time is further limited to the events of one week, or twenty-four hours, or even a few minutes. The screenwriter skillfully selects only the scope of the story that is needed to express the significant change (✗). All too often, beginning screenwriters are tempted to include far more time leading up to the event of change than the audience needs to know about. But experienced screenwriters have learned that the span of time immediately encompassing ✘ is important only to the degree that it has a direct cause-and-effect relationship with ✘.

Likewise, the skilled screenwriter collapses events, choosing only those incidents that directly impact the story and, more particularly, have an intrinsic connection to the ✘ that the story is about. Everyone knows, for instance, that characters in movies never have to take out their wallets and fish around for exactly the right taxi fare. They just grab a bill at random and hand it over to the cabbie. But, of course, the act of having the exact taxi fare is simply not important to the outcome of the drama. It has no bearing on the success or failure of the significant transition that the story is about.

On the other hand, such a mundane life event could have a crucial effect on the story if the writer chooses to make it so. We all know that, unlike real life, parking places abound in movies, and it is always possible to pull up directly outside the building the character is visiting. But in Robert Benton and David Newman's masterful script for *Bonnie and Clyde*, the screenwriters punch this staid convention in its nose to horrifying effect.

Bonnie, Clyde, and their dimwitted driver, C.W. Moss, pull into a small town square to rob the local bank. Small though the town may be, however, there's enough car and wagon traffic to prevent C.W. from parking. It hardly matters, because the robbery will take only a couple of minutes and then they'll be off again on their spree. However, while Bonnie and Clyde are inside the bank, C.W. spots a place being vacated. With great effort, and to the delight of both the audience and on-screen characters, he manages to shoehorn the car into the small gap. Unfortunately, when Bonnie and Clyde emerge from the bank, their getaway car is nowhere to be found! With a tremendous grinding of gears and jolting of bumpers, C.W. succeeds in extracting the car from its confinement while Bonnie and Clyde run to climb in. By now the furious bank manager has dashed out of the building and, as the getaway car careens around the corner, he leaps onto the running board.

5

Panicked by the unexpected events, Clyde spins around in the car and shoots the bank manager square in the face.

It is a chilling moment in the film, and the turning point of an inevitably tragic story that has, until this event, scrupulously avoided violence in favor of an almost lyrical romance. The scene of not being able to find a parking place *by itself* would have been meaningless, but the screenwriters accomplished a paradoxical shock to the audience's system by carefully selecting an event so ordinary as to seem comical, and then turning that event into the catastrophic linchpin of an ever-darkening drama.

THE SCREENPLAY PREMISE

By thoughtfully abbreviating the contiguous time of the story, and singling out only those events that have immediate influence on the success or failure of the life change of a character, the screenwriter develops a *premise*, that is, a brief statement of the central conflict of the story:

✓ Who is the main character?

✓ Who is the antagonist?

✓ What are they fighting about?

✓ What is the change that results from the conflict?

✓ Why must the main character take action to achieve the change?

It is this moral choice to act that the character must make which creates the *gestalt* and the sense of satisfaction and completeness that drama provides an audience, and that distinguishes a narratively compelling drama from the catalogue of random happenings that make up daily life.

Next, we'll look at the *audience-focused sequence* that grows from the premise and establishes the overall structure for a dramatic story—a beginning, middle, and end.

Scribble Exercise:

Write a three-sentence premise for your screenplay that details:

❏ One main character who acts against another character

Young woman leaves her live-in boyfriend (media type) b/c of deception —

❏ Why those characters must fight with each other to achieve a particular goal

They must fight to bring about the impetus for her to leave when she uncovers the deception

❏ How the main character's life changes because of the drama

The young woman changes internally becomes stronger, more confident + happy within herself + meets Someone wonderful.

8

Chapter Two

SATISFYING THE AUDIENCE

"There's nothing else. Just us, and the cameras, and those wonderful people out there in the dark."

— Norma Desmond in *Sunset Boulevard*

Whether around the fire, in a Greek amphitheater, on a medieval wagon, in an Elizabethan theater, or a modern multiplex movie house, humankind has been forever held in the thrall of a good storyteller. Sometimes the storyteller is a lone figure, sometimes a troupe of players, marionettes, animated cartoons, or major movie stars. But whether the story is told by a lone yarn spinner or the complex collaborative team required to make a movie, we in the audience have sat enraptured by tales that somehow illuminated our lives. Between the Bible, Greek mythology and drama, and the plays of William Shakespeare, the essential chronicles of humankind have all been told. Nevertheless, there are thousands of variations on these fundamental plots, and we seem to never tire of hearing the great stories retold over and over using various forms and characters.

How do the masters of the narrative art weave this magic? What special genius allows them to hold us in their power? Well, to be sure, there are some people who seem to be born dinner-table raconteurs, but most of us have to *learn* how to tell a good story. Moreover, a good writer always relearns and refines that skill continuously, acquiring an *earned instinct* for the shape of storytelling that captivates an audience.

The continual relearning means that nothing in this discussion of motion picture dramatic organization should be regarded as a formula. There is far too much mystery and magic in writing to reduce it to a formulaic act. Besides, formula storytelling is doomed to become repetitive and stale. Instead, we are looking at the *structure* of storytelling. Like the framework for a skyscraper or the armature for a sculptor's statue, it is the underlying structure of a screenplay that holds the weight of the story. Without a solid framework, the elements of the story have nowhere to live and will inevitably become irrelevant tidbits dangling in space.

Although it has been analyzed, condemned, twisted around, subdivided, and otherwise tortured for thousands of years, the essential dramatic structure consists of three acts:

✓ Act I   The Beginning   *meeting, the seduction*

✓ Act II   The Middle   *the relationship –*
high highs / low lows
doubts

✓ Act III   The End   *the betrayal*
+ end.

On the face of it, this three-act structure sounds so elementary as to seem ridiculously obvious, but then, a pyramid is also a pretty simple architectural structure, and no one questions its durability.

You probably learned a variation of this essential structure in any high school expository writing class. A paragraph has a topic sentence, a body, and a conclusion. And, of course, there's the old public-speaking maxim of *"Tell 'em what you're gonna tell 'em. Tell 'em. And tell 'em what you told 'em."* At its most basic, drama isn't very different from these time-honored principles of communicating information.

However, movie drama is more than just the communication of ideas. Movies are a highly emotional medium. They communicate to us through music, dialogue, sound effects, images, and a universe of tiny elements which make up a total experience that strikes more at our hearts than at our brains, our spirit more than our consciousness. A film script, then, is much more than mere notes for a speech or an outline for an essay. A good screenplay creates the foundation for a totality of experience that is virtually unknown outside of a movie theater, and the screenwriter's job is to lay down that structure as a *storyteller* who captivates the audience's soul.

So let's expand the definition of the three-act structure into a more *audience-focused* interpretation. Your job as a screenwriter is to take that *beginning*, *middle*, and *end* and transform them into

ATTRACTION   ANTICIPATION   SATISFACTION

We now have a vitality attached to the three acts and, moreover, an implied *purpose* for each of the segments.

ATTRACTION

In the beginning, the screenwriter attracts the audience's attention. We establish the main character, and present that character with a problem that must be resolved by reaching a clearly identifiable goal. Ideally the audience is interested in the character as a character. However, that interest is rarely sufficient by itself to undeniably capture the audience's attention. Their real attraction isn't so much to the character as to the predicament the character is in. The character may be flamboyant, colorless, adorable, or even mildly offensive, but it's the problem the character faces that attracts audience interest. Very early in Act I, the audience members need to say to themselves, *I want to see how the character gets out of this mess*. If you're successful as a screenwriter in getting your audience to make that commitment, then you're well on your way to telling a compelling story.

ANTICIPATION

In the middle, Act II, the screenwriter cranks up the tension of the story, heightening the audience's anticipation that more and more interesting things will happen. These interesting things aren't merely disjointed episodes and gags, however. They are events integrally related to the success or failure of the significant change that the drama is about. They are interesting to us in the context of the story because we want the character to succeed, but we can see that in order to do so, the character will have to overcome some formidable obstacles. In other words, the main character is forced by the *conflict* of drama to confront both an external antagonist and the main character's own internal fears.

SATISFACTION

Act III gives the audience satisfaction when the main character overcomes internal obstacles, resolves the external problem established in Act I, and reaches a worthy goal. The character thereby relieves the tension created through Act II, and sends the audience out of the theater content that they have seen a *gestalt*, a complete story. They may exit the theater happy or sad, exalted or outraged, laughing or crying—but they are *satisfied* that the story ended completely, that there were no ragged ends, and that for a brief two-hour time the world actually made sense.

Rain Man

1. Charlie Babbitt, a hard-driving, selfish young business hustler, discovers that his estranged father has willed a fortune to a brother Charlie never knew he had. *attraction*

2. Desperately in need of money to save his business, Charlie *anticipation* kidnaps his autistic savant brother, Raymond, effectively holding him for ransom to get a larger share of the inheritance. But as Charlie drives Raymond cross-country, he discovers that Raymond is able to calculate complicated mathematical problems in his head with great speed and accuracy. Charlie exploits Raymond's remarkable ability to win money in Las Vegas, but during their cross-country trip, Charlie gains something much more important—love for his brother, and recognition that Raymond is the imaginary "Rain Man" who protected Charlie during his childhood.

3. Abandoning his bitterness over the split with his father, Charlie focuses on retaining custody of Raymond, the brother he has come to love. But during the ultimate trusteeship hearing, it becomes clear that Raymond is not capable of living outside the institution where he has spent most of his life. Charlie has to give up his selfish goal for the good of his brother, but he has gained an understanding of himself and the ability to reach out to other people.

Scribble Exercise:

Write a *very brief* description of the action for each of the three acts of your screenplay.

❑ Act I   Attraction — young woman meets man who is exciting + seductive, but turns out to be deceptive + verbally cruel.

❑ Act II   Anticipation — chronicles the heyist lows of the relationship + final devastation of betrayal.

❑ Act III   Satisfaction — Woman garners strength to leave + make it on her own.

CHAPTER THREE

THE ELEMENTS OF SCREEN STORY

"We have to continually be jumping off cliffs and developing our wings on the way down."

— Kurt Vonnegut

To continue the architectural analogy of story structure as the standard three-act pattern, no matter how stable the framework is, our pyramid will crumble if it's assembled from flimsy materials. Virtually every story is constructed from certain building blocks that are necessary to establish the main character, the character's world, the problem that is at the core of the dramatic conflict, the possible solutions for that problem, and ultimately what the main character must do to overcome the obstacles and resolve the conflict.

Now, the exact order in which these building blocks are arranged is the craft of creative writing. In fact, often the blocks are chopped into smaller pieces and spread throughout the structure. In certain kinds (*genres*) of stories some of the building blocks may be larger or heavier or more prominent than others, while in a different variety of story those same blocks may be practically inconspicuous. Nevertheless, every well-constructed screen story will use *all* of these elemental building blocks because the elimination of any of them will weaken the overall structure and inevitably leave a gaping hole in the pyramid.

So, with the understanding that these elements of story do not have to come in the following order (although very often they will), let's examine the fundamental blocks that make up our edifice.

1. Back Story

If the story of significant change we want to tell occurs within the bounds of a selected and limited time, then obviously, something happened *before* this story began. Of course, many things happened, but in this case the ***back story*** refers to those events which establish the circumstances and setting for the current story that we are watching. Shakespeare's Prince Hamlet returns to Denmark, for instance, only to be confronted immediately by the ghost of his father, who tells Hamlet that his own mother and uncle are murderers, and commands Hamlet to avenge his death.

One of the most common errors which many beginning screenwriters make is that they feel compelled to include far too much back story in their screenplays. While the murder of the king and the scheming, illicit affair between Hamlet's mother Gertrude and his uncle Claudius may be interesting, Shakespeare wisely tells us only enough of that back story to establish the conditions for the play we are about to watch. We really don't need to know any more about the back story than is absolutely necessary for the far more interesting story of how Hamlet goes about resolving the dramatic conflict presented to him by the ghost.

Certainly you as the writer need to have a clear and sometimes even explicit idea of the back story, but the audience rarely needs much detail at all. We can be launched into the contemporary story with only the barest minimum of information, and often without any immediate back story information at all.

Depending on the genre and particular story a writer is telling, back story may be as obvious as Hamlet's dilemma or as complex and deliberately puzzling as the multiple back stories in Robert Towne's brilliant script for *Chinatown*. Although the detective story of *Chinatown* starts off simply enough with Jake Gittes accepting a routine divorce case, it escalates into a tangled maze of several back stories that twist around on each other. Jake himself has a personal back story; Evelyn Mulwray another; her father Noah Cross another; and even the City of Los Angeles comes with a contorted history all its own. But screenwriter Towne and director Roman Polanski feed the audience only bits and pieces of the necessary back stories as parts of the puzzle Jake must solve. This kind of continuous back story exposition is, in fact, a hallmark of detective films. It is the hidden back story that the detective must unravel in order to answer the puzzle presented by the dramatic conflict he's actually trying to resolve.

On the other hand, stories in some genres such as action-adventure often have very simple, uncomplicated back stories that can be presented in a line or two of dialogue. The opening voice-over narrative of James Cameron's *Terminator 2: Judgment Day* flatly states that there's a bad terminator coming to kill John Connor and a good terminator coming to rescue him: "It was only a question of which one got to him first." That's all we in the audience need to know to get the action started. We don't need a complete, detailed history of the future war or the motivations of the characters. We only need to know why things are about to happen—now let's get on with the show.

The least efficient and clumsiest way to present back story information to the audience is the *flashback narrative*. All too often beginning screenwriters want to stop the story the audience is watching and drop back in time to tell us a lengthy and usually unnecessary back story. By the time the audience is finished with this back story interruption, it

17

SCREENWRITING 101 / Hicks

has forgotten the contemporary story you're telling. Worse, you've lost whatever dramatic momentum you had built up to the point when you went to flashback.

To be sure, some deeply dramatic character dramas may require more back story to explain the complexity of relationships. A skillful screenwriter, however, keeps the back story to an absolute minimum. You should constantly ask yourself:

> ✓ Do we *really* need to know this back story information in order to tell the main story?
>
> ✓ What is the simplest, least obtrusive way to get the information to the audience?
>
> ✓ Is there a way I can give the audience the minimum necessary information while something else is happening? Can I keep the exposition in action so that the audience doesn't realize it's getting a back story?

If you examine the answers to these questions mercilessly, chances are you will find that you need much, much less back story than you initially thought you had to have.

2. Internal Need

Generally speaking, there are two kinds of back story: that which is strictly factual information, and that which emphasizes a subjective intuition about the main character. Detective, thriller, and action-adventure films, although also offering some insight into the state of being of the main character, tend to rely on the first kind of back story in order to set the conditions for the tale we are about to watch. More personal, relationship dramas, on the other hand, usually emphasize some missing personal quality that must be acquired by the main character.

[handwritten margin notes: internal need] the main charty... missing quality — chen d.n. recog. nece...]

In both of these kinds of back story, what is being established is an *internal need* for the main character. In order to be fully alive, the main character needs to come to grips with some personal attribute that he or she may not be completely aware of or may not be acknowledging. Often, in personal dramas, this missing attribute is a quality such as compassion or forgiveness or even self-reliance which the character believes he or she has but does not, or which the character simply does not recognize as necessary. Unknowingly, the character is going to be forced to deal with an internal, *vertical* significant change.

In more action-oriented dramas the quality may simply be courage or, more often, actual commitment to a value that the character has declared but never tested. The audience, however, normally has a sense of this missing personal quality, and part of what keeps us watching the story is the promise that the character will—in fact, *must*—acquire that quality in order for the dramatic conflict to be resolved to the audience's satisfaction.

It is the coming to grips with this internal need that provides more than merely a good tale for the audience. The resolution of the character's inner need provides us with a clarification of our own values and an exposition of our own frailties.

In *Rain Man*, for instance, the character of Charlie Babbitt has, because of events in his past relationship with his father, largely shut out the emotional part of himself. However, the drama we are watching will *force* Charlie to learn about and accept that emotional part of himself which he has been denying. In the classic action-adventure love story *The African Queen*, Charlie Allnut (Humphrey Bogart) has neatly explained away his avoidance of commitment to any person or any cause except himself, but the commencement of World War I and Charlie's love for Rosie (Katharine Hepburn) will *force* him into courageous self-sacrifice.

Beginning screenwriters often ask if the main character cannot simultaneously be the antagonist. The answer is that the main character is *always* the antagonist because the character has yet to battle the unknown of the internal need. However, without the pressure of outside dramatic circumstances and the threat of an external antagonist, the main character will never have to deal with the internal need. That painful battle has been successfully avoided so far, and the character will continue to ignore it unless forced into action by the insistence of the dramatic conflict.

3. Inciting Incident

So far we have a *back story* that presents us with a *main character* who has a hidden *internal need*, but nothing has yet happened in the story of significant change that we want to tell. Today must be like no other day in the character's life. Today something extraordinary is going to happen. Perhaps a war is going to start. Perhaps he's going to fall in love. Perhaps his long-lost brother is going to reappear. Perhaps he's going to be accidentally mistaken for someone else. Whatever it is, today there is an *inciting incident*, an unusual event that presents the main character with a problem to solve, challenge to overcome, or adventure to undertake. The main character is inescapably caught up in this inciting incident. The character cannot choose to ignore the consequences of the event and go on with life as if nothing had happened. Moreover, action is required now. The character cannot wait for the problem to disappear or someone else to solve it. Like it or not, the character is compelled to seek a solution to the problem or undertake the adventure that commands personal participation.

4. External Goal

The power of the inciting incident focuses the main character on an *external goal*, an action or object that the character believes will solve the problem presented by the inciting incident. At its simplest, the main character wants to achieve the goal in order to make life better. Making life better may be finding that special love, rescuing someone from danger, resolving the conflict with a family member, obtaining wealth, or saving the character's own life. Whatever it is, the character fixes on the external goal as the answer to the problem and we in the audience recognize the goal as something the character must achieve in order to resolve the dramatic conflict established by the inciting incident.

The timeless thriller *North by Northwest*, written by Ernest Lehman and directed by Alfred Hitchcock, contains the most elegantly simple inciting incident ever written for film. A perfectly unsuspecting advertising executive, played by Cary Grant, happens to stand up accidentally as a hotel page calls out the name of George Kaplan. This simple coincidence starts a chain reaction of mistaken identity, murder, and international intrigue that places the Cary Grant character into deeper and deeper jeopardy until he must take heroic action to extricate himself and the woman he's fallen in love with. It is clearly not a day like any other day, and because of it, the character will emerge from the dramatic conflict greatly changed from the person he was in the beginning.

5. Preparation

Achieving the external goal will not be easy for the main character. If it were easy, there would be no story. Ordinarily, the first thing the main character does is to devise a strategy for achieving the goal, gather resources and equipment, or assemble the necessary forces that will help achieve the goal. Depending on the story being told, the character may seek help from friends and family, professional helpers like police, or like-minded associates such as fellow soldiers. In *The Dirty Dozen*, for instance, the bulk of the film is about preparing a bunch of criminal misfits to act together as a military unit in order to achieve the goal. Conversely, the element of *preparation* may be strictly individual as well. In the original *Rocky*, Rocky Balboa undergoes intense, solitary physical and mental training for his upcoming fight with Apollo Creed, and in both *Ordinary People* and *Good Will Hunting*, the main characters prepare for their upcoming battles through difficult revelations in psychotherapy.

21

No matter what kind of story you are telling, though, the period of preparation must be dramatic; that is, the preparation itself has a profound effect on the main character, and may be the element which causes the character to come to grips with the internal need.

6. Opposition

Just the fact that a character has a problem to solve by reaching a goal does not make the story dramatic, however. Remember that drama is *conflict*. Without opposition, there is no tension or expectation built up for the audience. Every drama requires an outside force that is trying to prevent the main character from reaching his goal. For the most part, this force of opposition takes the form of a personified antagonist—another person who has either the same goal as the main character or a goal that is mutually exclusive.

Moreover, the antagonist is necessarily bigger and more powerful, and has more resources than the main character. If the antagonist is not more powerful than the main character, there is no opposition. The main character simply brushes past the antagonist and reaches his goal with no interference. Antagonists need not always be *evil*, but they have a goal that conflicts with the goal of the main character. Professor Lambeau in *Good Will Hunting* is certainly not evil. In fact he has, he believes, Will's best interest at heart. Nevertheless, he is the antagonist because his goal for Will is contradictory to Will's external goal for himself. Because the antagonist is more powerful than the main character, then, all the main character's planning and preparation necessarily fails. He is *apparently defeated*. All the favorable options have been eliminated. The main character is left with no resources except *himself*.

7. Self-Revelation

It is at this lowest point in the drama that the main character comes to grips with the internal need, and therefore undergoes an internal significant change because of the pressures of the external dramatic conflict.

This revelation may be expressed in dialogue to another character, but it is generally more effective for the audience to see the effect of the self-revelation rather than to imagine the character's internal transformation. In fact, set yourself a rule when writing: A character never *realizes*. The audience realizes based on what the character *does*.

8. Obsession

Now, as a changed person, one who has had some personal revelation, the main character focuses even more intently on the external goal. Remember that the external goal never had anything to do directly with the character's internal need, so whatever was at stake in the original problem is still unresolved. The external goal becomes even more important for both the main character and the antagonist, and unless the main character achieves the goal, a great deal will be lost. That is, the main character is now fighting to achieve the external, lateral significant change ← ✗ → of the plot that affects the surrounding society, (( )) including those of us in the audience.

9. Battle

Compromise between the main character and the antagonist is now impossible. They cannot both obtain their goals, so they *must* fight, and only one can win. Depending on the story you are telling, the *battle* may be a physical confrontation like the gunfight in the dusty western street, or it may be a verbal battle in a courtroom, or perhaps an emotional set-to between estranged lovers or family members. In any case, the only way the original dramatic conflict can be settled, and the audience's tension thereby relieved, is for the protagonist and antagonist to fight *to the death*, whether that death is literal or figurative. It is important to remember here that we have been watching a story about a main character, and it is that main character who must fight for his own salvation. It would be unwise and very unsatisfying to an audience to bring in an outside force at this point to save the main character. He must be responsible for extracting himself from the predicament, or the self-revelation forced by the external events of the drama has been meaningless.

It is also important to recognize as a screenwriter that the audience has invested its emotions and its time in wanting the main character to achieve his goal and win. Often, beginning screenwriters want to kill their main characters, believing that the death of the protagonist is somehow more meaningful. Although there are certainly some great movies in which the main character dies at the end, such as *Saving Private Ryan*, they are stories where the character dies for a noble cause that is more worthy than the original external goal. The audience can be satisfied that while the hero may have been killed, his death served a purpose that made the surrounding society safer or more complete. Generally, however, killing your main character is a very risky technique because it disregards the audience's expectations for the drama and dedication to the main character.

10. Resolution

The main character solves the conflict established by the inciting incident and moves on to a new story. Both the main character and the surrounding society have been *significantly changed* by the events of this story. It is possible that the degree of internal change for the main character is profound while the degree of change for the surrounding society of family and friends is comparatively minor, as occurs in many intensely personal dramas. But more likely, the internal change that the main character has been forced to undergo has allowed that character to make a momentous change in the surrounding society, whether that society is a fragile western town, a country at war, or a threatened civilization. The character may go on to live a sedate life, or he may continue as a champion, but he will never again be the person he was in the beginning of the drama. Because of the character's actions, the surrounding world has been forever altered.

Again, these ten story elements should not be regarded as a formula or a fill-in-the-blanks. They are fundamental principles of storytelling that help create a tight, overall structure. These elements need not inevitably appear in your screenplay in this particular order, nor with equal weight, depending on the particular story you want to tell. However, *all* of these elements will be present in any well-constructed screen story, and as you gain more experience writing, you will internalize these principles so that, although you may not consciously be thinking about them, they will become integral parts of every screenplay you write.

For now, simply use this list as a tool to help you think about the events you need to include in your screenplay. Just listen to your writer's intuition and jot down your thoughts and impressions for each element in the Scribble Exercise that follows without trying to be too detailed.

Scribble Exercise:

Write a brief statement describing each of the elements of story structure for your screenplay.

❑ Back Story *happy, popular, recently grad moves to NYC determined to be a doctor*

❑ Internal Need *— wants to find love, security*

❑ Inciting Incident *— meets seductive, "exciting" man who promises the world*

❑ External Goal *become d.*

❏ Preparation — vigorously attends classes, works her

❏ Opposition (Antagonist)

❏ Self-Revelation

❏ Obsession

❏ Battle

❏ Resolution

CHAPTER FOUR

SCREEN CHARACTERS

"Things in motion sooner catch the eye
Than what not stirs."

— William Shakespeare

The mortar that holds these story element blocks in place is **character**. In truth, it is impossible to separate plot (story) from character because one cannot exist without the other. Even those films which purport to be *character* movies, with little or no overt action, still have a story of some sort. As we've seen, plot is the story of significant change for a character, and that character's actions cause a story about significant change for a surrounding world. You can't have one without the other.

Nevertheless, many books on dramatic writing will provide some version of a fill-in-the-blanks list for creating character. These check-off forms usually ask questions about the physical, psychological, and social traits of character such as

✓ What color is your character's hair?

✓ How tall is your character?

✓ What is your character's occupation?

✓ What is your character's attitude toward sex?

✓ etc.

All of these inventories of traits, however, are intended to help you *build* a character, as if we could take hair color from one column, height from another, occupation from another, etc., and come up with an interesting character by authorial cut and paste. But characters are far more than mere catalogues of attributes. They are living, breathing beings that inhabit your screenplay. They provide vitality in what is otherwise an inert scaffolding, and they are the glue that hold together the bricks of structure.

The best screenplays are not inhabited by characters that are *built*. Creative screenwriters recognize that characters are alive and complete the instant you conceive of them. They live within you, and your job is to find ways that will allow them to come out. In this sense, writing is a metaphysical invocation of character. You must become a discoverer of character, not a creator. In a sense, you are like the medium at a séance table, summoning your characters to take part in the drama that's growing in your creative imagination.

Now this may seem a little supernatural to those who come to the screen from more reportorial forms of writing, but for all the rules of structure that screenwriting obeys, it is not a formula, and worthy characters cannot be fabricated in order to be exploited in some indifferent plot.

Instead, the writer must listen to the inner voice— not the writer's inner voice, but the voice of the character within the writer.

✓ **Learn to listen actively**. Let your characters talk to you. There is no more heady experience for a writer than not being able to type fast enough to get your characters' words down on paper. Characters do take on lives of their own if you don't force them. Trust your characters' instincts.

✓ **Use your autobiographical lens**. Now, of course, all characters are *you*. Who else could they be? You may say that

30

you're basing a character on cousin Suzy, but the truth is you're invoking a character with *Suzyness* filtered through your own autobiographical lens. To make full use of the lens, you must get in touch with your own feelings, doubts, fears, elation, and disappointments. And remember that the lens works from both sides. Very often when you have a character that simply refuses to act or talk or behave, a character that sits in the middle of the screenplay like a sodden lump, the chances are that the character is *too much you*. You're trying to write too autobiographically, trying to include too much of your self in the character. If that is the case, find a quality in your character that is *more* than you. If your character is selfish, for instance, get in touch with how difficult it is to buy your sister an expensive birthday present; then magnify that feeling, press it through the lens until it infuses the character. The character will take on a life of its own and suddenly surprise you with very un-you actions.

✓ Lastly, to invoke rather than build characters, you must fall in love with them. Characters are not perfect any more than flesh-and-blood people are, but you must nevertheless fall in love with them. You cannot be merely interested in them or curious about them—you must *love* them.

So, having condemned lists, let's look at a list that will help you invoke character.

Scribble Exercise:

Respond to the following questions without *thinking* about them. There are no correct answers. It's your immediate, gut reaction that counts, not any carefully crafted response. In fact, it might be a good idea to have someone else read these questions to you aloud so that you can't *cheat*.

❑ When was your main character happiest? *Performing in plays as a child*

❑ What talent would your main character most like to have? *acting, dancing*

❑ If your main character could change one thing about him- or herself, what would it be? *Higher self-esteem, greater self-confidence.*

❑ What does your main character consider to be his or her greatest achievement? *Friends + family rel'ships*

❏ What is your main character's most treasured possession?

Wedding ring

❏ What is your main character's greatest extravagance?

Dining out

❏ When does your main character lie?

To protect others' feelings

❏ What is your main character's greatest regret?

Not "going for it" w/ acting / professionally

Any surprises?

If none of your answers surprised you, then you're trying to control your character too tightly. Let the character breathe. Allow yourself to discover rather than manufacture your character.

So, let's go on a character discovery journey. Below is the map (okay, it's another list), and the premise that you wrote for your screenplay in Chapter One should answer these questions:

WHO IS YOUR MAIN CHARACTER?

WHAT DOES THE MAIN CHARACTER WANT?

WHAT'S STOPPING THE MAIN CHARACTER FROM
REACHING THE GOAL?

WHO IS YOUR MAIN CHARACTER?

The conventional roll call of physical, social, and psychological traits actually deceives screenwriters because it ignores the most important substance of screen characters. Characters are what they *do*. If drama is conflict, character is action. Now, action doesn't necessarily mean gunfights and car chases. Action means that the characters do something to achieve the goal; they make a series of dramatic choices. By definition, a dramatic choice is one that involves conflict. For example, in the screenplay for *The Verdict*, written by David Mamet, Frank Galvin is a drunken, failed attorney who has a chance to settle a medical malpractice case out of court for a large sum of money. However, when Frank is actually presented with the check, he refuses to make the deal. "If I take that money I'm lost. I'm just going to be a rich ambulance chaser." It is a crucial, dramatic decision that sets the course of action for the remainder of the story.

34

In the feature film *The Fugitive*, Dr. Kimble is recaptured after his awesome escape from the train wreck, but when presented with the choice of submitting to the orders of Marshal Samuel Gerard or leaping to his almost certain death over the spillway, Kimble makes the leap. Not every character in every situation will have to make such a life-threatening choice, but the decisions they make should be equally dramatic within the context of their story.

Scribble Exercise:

❑ What is the first *dramatic choice* your main character makes?

Stay after 1st deception

❑ Why is your main character *required* to make that choice rather than taking some easier option?

❑ What is the immediate result of the dramatic choice the main character makes?

❑ What other characters are affected by the main character's dramatic choice?

CHARACTERS' MINIMUM ACTION

Characters make choices based on their beliefs about themselves and the way they think and behave—the internal need story element. But characters don't instinctively make *dramatic* decisions. Like everyday humans, characters take the *minimum* action necessary so as not to risk betrayal of their internal need.

Imagine the character of Stanley, a bashful, reserved accountant who has just purchased a new house. On his first night in the new home he discovers that the large dog next door barks loudly and monotonously, making it impossible for Stanley to get any sleep. What does Stanley choose to do in order to remedy the situation?

Given the kind of character Stanley is, that is—who he believes himself to be and how he has chosen to act in the past—Stanley will most likely pull the pillow over his head and try to shut out the noise. But the dog continues to bark. After a second sleepless night, perhaps he calls the police or the animal control department, neither of which will do him much good in a large city. After three nights of sleeplessness, Stanley may be desperate enough to sneak next door and slip an anonymous note in the neighbor's mail box: *Please quiet your dog.* Chances are, this courageous act will go unanswered. Stanley becomes a nervous wreck. He hasn't had a good night's sleep for a week. Once again, just as his head hits the pillow, the dog sets up its nightly howl. Stanley, now in desperation, anger, or recklessness, throws on his robe and resolutely stalks across the lawn to pound on the neighbor's door. One way or another, he's going to stop that damned dog from barking! But, the front door is opened by the most gorgeous, scantily clad woman Stanley has ever seen. She offers him a martini and invites him to come inside and keep her company on the sofa. Now Stanley has to make a difficult, dramatic choice.

But Stanley only reached the difficult decision because he first tried all the easy steps. It would be thoroughly out of character for Stanley to

37

initially take the dramatic choice of direct confrontation with the neighbor. He had to be driven to that action by process of elimination.

A clever screenwriter, however, will force Stanley to the dramatic action more quickly without losing credibility. What if, for instance, it had been established on Stanley's first night that a crucially important business meeting would be held the following morning, and that Stanley's entire future career depended on his alertness at that meeting? Faced with the possible ruin of his professional life, Stanley might well be willing to risk his personal self-concept in a bold showdown.

It is the character's ***self-concept*** that makes up the ***who*** of our map. In part, the self-concept is what we might call the ***attitude***, the way a character wants to be perceived by the world, or believes he or she is perceived by the world. A distinctive temperament is often embodied by star actors. Stars are, in fact, just that—actors who somehow personify a certain demeanor on-screen. Think of Cary Grant, Jimmy Stewart, Arnold Schwarzenegger, or Harrison Ford. Certainly they are great actors, but they are movie stars because no matter what role they play they fill that role with the powerful image of themselves. Audiences go to see a Clint Eastwood movie because they know more or less who they're going to see Clint Eastwood be. Now this is not to take anything away from Mr. Eastwood as a actor, but no one seriously expects to see him play Stanley the accountant, or even the tortured, doubting Hamlet for that matter, because Eastwood has made a career largely out of being a rugged, coldly determined character. In the audience we would probably be very uncomfortable watching Clint Eastwood vacillate and stammer his way through a role.

Most of the time a screenwriter will have no choice about the casting of a script, but you can make use of this star temperament as a tool for allowing a character to reveal himself. If, for instance, you picture Clint Eastwood as your star, think about what it is besides commercial

appeal that makes "Eastwoodness" indicative of your main character. By analyzing what makes that actor seem right for the part, you may find a key to the attitude your character has about himself in relation to the world. Attitude is a character quality that you must write into the script.

More important from the screenwriter's point of view are the *values* that make up the character's self-concept. Consider Rick, the Humphrey Bogart character in *Casablanca*, for a moment. We'd have to say that Rick's attitude is cynical, a tough-guy bystander watching life's struggle. Yet, as the movie unfolds, it is Rick's values that are tested. His attitude remains that of a tough guy, but he also reveals a deeply held value system which seems to be at odds with the tough-guy image.

Values are the beliefs and opinions about the forces that shape life which the character has incorporated into his image of himself—and it is exactly these values that are going to be challenged by the external events of the story, thereby making the character come to grips with the internal need and alter the self-concept.

Captain Frank Ramsey (Gene Hackman) and Lieutenant Commander Hunter (Denzel Washington) in *Crimson Tide*, written by Michael Schiffer and Richard P. Henrick, are good examples of characters who battle over opposed self-concepts, that is, contrary value systems. They both serve their country and they both want to do the right thing. Neither man is evil, but their individual value systems make each of them question how to go about doing the right thing, and that is the stuff of the dramatic conflict. In the end, both officers have to expose their internal needs and adjust their self-concepts, though on the face of it neither seems to have changed his attitude at all.

In *Good Will Hunting*, Will Hunting is clearly in turmoil because he has managed to construct a self-concept that allows him to deny his internal need. Yet, because of the conflict of the drama, Will Hunting must painfully adjust his self concept, exposing his hidden fears in order to free himself from the value systems imposed by two competing societies. One of the clearest examples of this kind of self-revelation, of course, occurs in L. Frank Baum's classic story for the film *The Wizard of Oz*, when Dorothy confesses, "...if I ever go looking for my heart's desire again, I won't look any further than my own backyard. Because if it isn't there, I never really lost it to begin with!"

THEORY OF COGNITIVE DISSONANCE

There is a useful tool called the *Theory of Cognitive Dissonance*,[1] by Leon Festinger, that you can borrow from psychology to help reveal characters' self-concepts. Dissonance theory is too complicated to discuss in detail here, but, to flagrantly paraphrase Festinger, a person will experience discomfort (dissonance) whenever faced with two or more contradictory bits of knowledge (cognitions) about himself or the environment. Remember that characters act; that is, they make decisions. Their choices are dramatic because of the potential for cognitive dissonance, that is, for *self-doubt*.

If you have ever had to make a difficult decision between two basically equal purchases, you've experienced cognitive dissonance. Let's say you set out to buy a car. You can buy a Ford or a Chevrolet. Each costs exactly $20,000, and each is identically equipped. Barring any mythology that may accompany each brand, they are virtually identical in every respect—but you can only buy one of them. Finally, after agonizing over the decision, you write a check for the ... Ford. Cognitive dissonance theory says that you will immediately begin to doubt the choice you made. In the absence of any other information, you will wish you'd bought the Chevrolet.

Furthermore, dissonance theory says you will actively avoid situations and information that would likely increase dissonance. Stanley, our

[1] Leon Festinger, *A Theory of Cognitive Dissonance*, Stanford University Press, 1962.

bashful accountant, is not going to immediately rush next door and throttle the barking dog with his bare hands. To even think of such a thing would be out of Stanley's character. To actually do it would be impossible—unless a compelling rival cognition makes the unthinkable act conceivable. Faced with losing his job, and thereby devastating a huge chunk of his self-concept, or risking a midnight rumble and a lesser part of his self-concept, Stanley opts for the doggy confrontation. Except, Stanley hedges his bet. The hand-to-fang battle of accountant and Doberman is too much for Stanley's self-concept to adjust to, so he elects to risk his personality with the owner instead. And now, the screenwriter throws Stanley the biggest curve of his shy life, the inciting incident that makes today unlike any other day. By avoiding the flesh-eating, saber-toothed canine, Stanley has set himself up for a negligee-clad beauty who's going to mutilate his self-concept beyond all recognition.

In fact, let's carry this story forward just a bit. Stanley and Suzy Centerfold fall head-over-heels in love. They shop in the open-air market, ride a tandem bicycle, and feed the animals at the zoo. It is obvious to the audience that these two unlikely sweethearts are meant for each other.

Or is it? However much we in the audience may want the satisfaction of seeing Stanley and Suzy unite, we also perceive something that the characters are too busy to notice. The lovers clearly are not meant for each other because their individual self-concepts are so radically contrary that for the two of them to actually wind up together would be completely incredible. The audience understands, even if the characters do not, that both of these characters are going to have to make some changes before they can truly get together.

Indeed, one day while running in slow motion down the beach, the characters are slammed up against their individual self-concepts. Stanley is gripped with panic. *I'm an accountant. I like classical music. What am I doing with a gorgeous centerfold who listens to Elvis Presley*

41

songs? And Suzy is no different. Her self-concept rears its exquisitely coifed head and declares it could never be linked to some puny nerd who doesn't even recognize *Jailhouse Rock* as the screen classic that it is. Alas, boy and girl repel each other.

Yet it is the parting of the lovers that will force each of these characters to deal with their internal needs, to confront their self-concepts, and rush back into each other's arms as changed people with the capacity to be fully alive in their love. And it is this mutual revision of self-concepts that makes the story ultimately satisfying for the audience. The characters had to learn how to overcome obstacles to reach the reward of having each other. Virtually every love story, albeit with greatly differing characters, follows this same general pattern. Characters' self-concepts will not be denied, and the screenwriter who ignores this fundamental truth does so at the peril of creating a disconcerting, unsatisfying story.

CONFLICT FOCUS

The key to a character's revelation of internal need—to the confrontation with the self-concept—is, of course, the external conflict of the drama. The self-concept is so thoroughly protected and accounted for that a character will never change. In the words of cognitive dissonance theory, a person *will actively avoid situations and information which would likely increase dissonance.* In other words, it will take a momentous opposition set off by the inciting incident to compel the character to make the difficult choices that threaten his or her self-concept.

Broadly there are five kinds of dramatic conflict that provide the impetus for dramatic change in the character and the surrounding society: intrapersonal, interpersonal, situational, social, and relational.

    1. **Intrapersonal** conflict focus is the character mired in self-doubt. These "Long Day's Journey into Despair" films have

the least dramatic conflict focus because, while the character's pain may indeed be agonizing, the very fact that the conflict is locked inside the character makes for an inertia that is not cinematic; that is, the character simply sits and suffers while we in the audience have very little to watch. Frequently these films, such as *The Prince of Tides*, are adapted from highly interior novels and require very burdensome literary techniques such as voice-over narrative and long historical flashbacks to keep the dramatic conflict alive.

2. **Interpersonal** conflict focus is more dramatic because the internal apprehensions of a character are played out against another, often closely related, character. These kinds of dramas can be compelling in their emotional turmoil, but are customarily not so much movies as they are filmed stage plays. *Marvin's Room, Ordinary People, Terms of Endearment*, and even *Driving Miss Daisy* are examples of these kinds of one-room dramas that are commonly precipitated by imminent funerals, incurable diseases, weddings, or other pressured family reunions where the characters thrash about in emotional wrestling matches until they have resolved the long-standing conflict between them.

3. **Situational** conflict focus involves opposition from natural forces, as in the films *Earthquake, The Towering Inferno, Volcano*, and *Twister*. Ostensibly the drama is about whether or not the characters can escape the burning building during the earthquake before the tornado destroys them. But the fact is that burning buildings, earthquakes, and tornadoes have no will. They just do what natural forces do, completely without any antagonistic intent and totally unaware of the characters they affect. The outcome of the conflict, then, is a simple *either-or* proposition—either the characters live or they don't. There may be physical strength and ingenuity demanded of the characters for them to survive, but there is no serious challenge to

43

their self-concepts because no moral consequence is at stake. Neither the characters nor the surrounding society will be much affected by the disaster story. Instead, interpersonal conflict provides the real drama within the context of the situational crisis. The actual dramatic story for *Twister*, for instance, is the relationship between Bill Harding, played by Bill Paxton, and Jo Harding, played by Helen Hunt. For all of its whiz-bang special effects, the twister has no real dramatic impact except as an external circumstance that brings the two estranged lovers back together again to work out their unfinished personal relationship.

The awkwardness of situational conflict is not limited to action-adventure films. In the comedy classic *Mr. Blandings Builds His Dream House*, written by Melvin Frank and Norman Panama, Jim and Muriel Blandings (Cary Grant and Myrna Loy) decide to retreat from their crowded Manhattan apartment by converting a quaint, hundred-year-old Connecticut farmhouse. As in the later film it inspired, *The Money Pit*, the Blandings's dream house becomes a comedic ordeal of hugely expensive construction and renovation disasters.

The apparent external goal of the film, obviously, is for the Blandings to overcome all the remodeling obstacles and complete their dream house. However, the structural difficulty with this goal is that it requires what is essentially the same event to be repeated over and over again. There is qualitatively no difference between the problems of having to drill a new well and the problems of having to pump out the flooded basement. Like escape from the burning skyscraper or fleeing the onslaught of volcanic lava, these either-or events quickly lose any dramatic value. Mr. Blandings' house has no more conscious determination than the tornado or the volcano. The antics of solving the problems may be enjoyable or exciting, but they are not *dramatic*.

However, as anyone who has ever remodeled a house can testify, the stresses of such a venture put an enormous strain on a marriage, and it is here that the real dramatic conflict of the story plays out. An evidently happy couple, the underpinnings of the Blandings' marriage require as much renovation as the new house they're constructing. The real dramatic goal, which is carried in a subplot about jealousy, is the restoration of a strong bond between Jim and Muriel—a goal the audience instinctively recognizes as being the true, worthy external goal of the story. Meanwhile, there is also a tertiary conflict worrying Jim at his Manhattan advertising agency, but you'll have to see the film to find out how he solves that problem.

4. **Social** conflict focus occurs between a person and a group. Often this kind of drama is about a conflict of cultural or socio-political values, as in *Full Metal Jacket*, *The Killing Fields*, or *Boyz N the Hood*. The awkwardness of social conflict drama is that socio-political and cultural attitudes are so amorphous that it is difficult for the main character to fight against anything specific enough to force self-revelation. The social conflict drama, then, usually requires a personified antagonist to represent the values of the group. In *Boyz N the Hood*, for instance, there is the ever-present specter of the gang members cruising the neighborhood. They are the personification of the malignancy that Tre has the opportunity to break free of, if only he can find the inner strength to overcome their distorted seduction. In *Full Metal Jacket*, written by Gustav Hasford, Michael Herr, and Stanley Kubrick, the conflict becomes appallingly personal when Joker has to administer the coup de grâce at close range to an agonizingly wounded teenage Vietnamese sniper. The elegantly simple commemoration for both the end of her life and Joker's action comes from another Marine, "Hard core, man. Fucking hard core."

45

5. **Relational** conflict focus is the most common and the most credible—a direct confrontation with an antagonist who has a mutually exclusive goal. In order to achieve the external goal, the main character is forced into active self-revelation. In the classic screenplay for *Casablanca* by Julius and Philip Epstein and Howard Koch, Rick's love for Ilsa and his loyalty to freedom is directly tested by Major Strasser. Rick cannot fight the entire Nazi regime, but he can take one small action for the cause of freedom. To do so, however, requires a major self-sacrifice and confrontation with the uninvolved cynic that he has made himself out to be with his now famous speech, "I'm no good at being noble, but it doesn't take much to see that the problems of three little people don't amount to a hill of beans in this crazy world."

In a totally different kind of movie, the relational conflict between the "good" Terminator, played by Arnold Schwarzenegger, and Robert Patrick's "bad" T-1000 even forces androids to have self-realization when the Terminator declares, "I know now why you cry, though it is something I can never do."

No matter which kind of conflict focus your story generates, it is the external opposition that forces the main character to make a significant life change, by which we in the audience learn something about ourselves. It is this clarity of vision brought about through the drama that makes the experience *satisfying*. Now, this does not mean that the screenwriter sets out to preach to the audience. There is nothing more excruciating than a movie that is designed to teach us a lesson. We come into the theater to be entertained, not propagandized, but intentionally or not, we also expect to be enlightened. That is what the experience of drama is about—a shared experience that makes the world a bit more understandable.

WHAT DOES THE MAIN CHARACTER WANT?

The inciting incident establishes for the main character an external goal, something to be achieved that the character believes will make life better. The external goal may be money, love, saving the life of a child, saving one's own life, resolving a relationship, or hundreds of other specific accomplishments that the character believes unquestionably must be attained.

Whatever the external goal, it needs to meet two tests.

1. **The external goal must be identifiable to the audience**. If the audience does not know why the character is acting, they will be completely lost. The audience does not have to agree that the goal is worthy, but they must know what the character's objective is.

In *Rain Man*, written by Ron Bass, for example, Charlie Babbitt's external goal is to acquire money to keep his business from failing. The method he chooses to get the money is to essentially kidnap his brother and hold him for ransom. The audience recognizes intrinsically that Charlie's goal is ultimately not an admirable one, but it is nonetheless quite clear, and without the goal of acquiring money, none of the remainder of the drama happens at all.

2. **The external goal must be relevant to the audience beyond the audience's identification with the character**. Something must be at stake that the audience can *feel*. They must recognize that a great deal will be lost if the main character does not achieve the goal. In other words, the audience must sense a threat to their own existence. Now, the threat may not be lethal. Perhaps it's a sense of threat to their well-being, or their perception of how the world works, or their notion of justice, but whatever the threat is, it must connect to

47

the audience directly beyond their mere identification with the character's plight.

In the thriller *Breakdown*, written by Jonathan Mostow and Sam Montgomery, for instance, the character, Jeff Taylor, played by Kurt Russell, mysteriously loses his wife while driving cross-country. It becomes increasingly evident that she has been taken by a group of ruthless kidnappers. Certainly the audience identifies with the plight of Jeff Taylor in the movie, but more significant, they recognize inherently that their own worst nightmares are being played out in Taylor's story. They are intensely engaged in the story precisely because of the it-could-happen-to-me feeling.

Scribble Exercise:

❏ What is your main character's *specific* external goal?

❏ Is this initial external goal replaced by a different *external* goal (not the *internal* need)?

❏ How is the external goal made clearly identifiable to the audience?

❏ How is the external goal relevant to the audience? What will the audience lose if the main character does not reach the goal?

THE HIERARCHY OF BASIC NEEDS

There is another concept from psychology that you may find useful in determining your character's external goal: Abraham Maslow's *Hierarchy of Basic Needs**. Maslow's theory is that there are certain things human beings strive for, and they must secure these things in a specific order or hierarchy. In fact, Maslow says, without satisfying the lower order of the hierarchy, it is impossible to achieve the next stage. As it happens, there are certain kinds of films, or genres, whose external goals can be illustrated by Maslow's hierarchy of needs.

1. **Physiological Needs** - food, water, air, shelter, sex—those things without which we cannot live. Except for pure survival-against-nature films, we don't often make movies with physiological needs as the chief external goal. As we discussed with situational conflict focus, the issue of survival, although certainly identifiable to the audience, is not as dramatic as the human relational drama that occurs within the survival context. One possible exception to this tendency might be the inclusion of money as a primary physiological need since, for most of us, money is necessary to acquire the elements of survival. However, the amount of money that usually appears in films as an external goal far surpasses any quantity required for strictly staying alive.

2. **Safety Needs** - security, stability, order, protection, and freedom from fear or danger. Obviously, a great many films are made where safety is the primary external goal. Thriller stories, in fact, require that the main character be powerfully motivated to save his own life, regardless of whatever else may be at stake. And of all the external goals, safety may be the most easily identifiable to an audience. Movies are an emotional medium, and fear is an emotion that promptly grabs an audience by its throat.

---

* Maslow Abraham. *Motivation and Personality*, Harper & Row, New York, 1970.

3. **Social Needs** - love, acceptance, belongingness. The intrapersonal and interpersonal dramas, including comedy and happily-ever-after fantasies, always have love and belongingness as the primary external goal. Characters in these stories are trying to be fully alive by reaching out for acceptance to other characters.

4. **Ego Needs** - esteem, reputation, self-respect, status. Many action films such as *Heat*, written by Michael Mann, focus on the impact of the characters' self-conflict, or ego drive. At one point in the story, Neil, the professional thief, announces to Vincent, the professional cop, "I do what I do best. I take down scores. You do what you do best. Try to take guys like me." It is the summation of their lives and they both agree that neither of them knows how or wants to do anything else.

In one way or another, most comedy stories tend to be about characters achieving fame or success, sometimes in spite of themselves, from Buster Keaton's *The General*, where a railroad engineer bumbles his way into becoming an unlikely war hero, to *Tootsie*, written by Larry Gelbart and Murray Schisgal, where Michael the unsuccessful actor so desperately needs to feed his ego that he succeeds in passing himself off as a woman.

However, there are also interpersonal dramas that go beyond mere esteem into the realm of metaphysical worthiness, such as Woody Allen's *Crimes and Misdemeanors*, and Peter Shaffer's *Amadeus*, when Salieri rails against God, "He gave me that longing--then made me mute. Why?...Tell me that? If he didn't want me to serve him with music, why implant the desire--like a lust in my body--then deny me the talent?"

5.   **Self-Actualization Needs**—creativity, self-expression, personal fulfillment. These films tend to be about directly serving a community, or finding a personal quality such as integrity. As an external goal, self -actualization is, perhaps, the most difficult to portray dramatically because so much of the *action* occurs inside the character. It is necessary, therefore, to play the main character off against a functional antagonist so that the audience can see the internal workings of the character, as in *Dead Man Walking*, written by Tim Robbins from Sr. Helen Prejean's book, when Matthew Poncelet has the impertinence to compare himself to Jesus. Prejean flares, "No, man, not a whole lot like you. Jesus changed the world with his love. You watched while two kids were murdered."

Scribble Exercise:

❏ Using the hierarchy of basic needs as a guide, what is missing in your main character's life that must be achieved in the film story?

❏ Are there primary goals the character must fulfill on screen before the character seeks out the external goal? That is, will the audience sense something out of place if the character seeks glory, for instance, when he doesn't have enough food to feed his family?

WHAT'S STOPPING THE MAIN CHARACTER FROM REACHING THE GOAL?

The protagonist, or main character, of a story can only be as compelling as the **antagonist** forces him to be. That is, the main character will only do what he must do to get what he wants, therefore the intensity of the antagonist must drive the main character to take action. In practice, this means that you must ask the same questions of the antagonist that you do of the protagonist. The only difference between them is that the antagonist acts from an irreconcilable moral ethos. The antagonist has, in other words, a different self-concept.

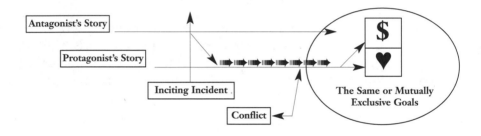

Consider that the antagonist's plan is well in effect by the time the protagonist enters the story.

Because of the inciting incident, the main character thrusts into the antagonist's story, intruding on the antagonist's plans, and forcing the antagonist to divert energy to the defeat of the protagonist, thereby creating the dramatic conflict that is the story of significant change.

The irreconcilable moral ethos is easy to see in action-adventure, detective, thriller, and even comedy films. In *Independence Day*, written by Dean Devlin and Roland Emmerich, for example, the invading aliens clearly state that they want the people of Earth to die, and they do a pretty good job of reaching their goal. Were it not for the hearty and resourceful band of remaining humans, the Earth would belong to the aliens. But the humans are driven to achieve their goal, driven beyond what they may have believed they were capable of in the beginning of the story.

In love stories and other interpersonal dramas the antagonist may not be so easily identifiable because the opposition is rarely outright evil. Rather, the antagonist in an interpersonal relationship story acts to defend a different self-concept that is threatened by association with the main character. Perhaps the antagonist is the opposite lover, or the estranged sister, or even the main character's mother as in *Ordinary People*. And, in some cases, the antagonist, while not personally corrupt, represents a societal point of view that is the antithesis of the main character's goal. In *Good Will Hunting*, written by Ben Affleck and Matt Damon, Professor Lambeau genuinely believes he has Will's welfare at heart, and from his point of view he is perfectly correct in his goal for the young genius, "Don't infect him with the idea that it's ok to quit. That it's ok to be a failure, because it's not ok!"

Scribble Exercise:

Who is the antagonist in:

❏ The Silence of the Lambs?

❏ Titanic?

❏ The Piano?

In *The Verdict*, Frank Galvin, the character played by Paul Newman, is opposed in court by Edward Concannon, played by James Mason. Concannon is not *evil*, but his stated goal is to "win the case," which is exactly the same goal Frank Galvin has. Edward Concannon happens to be on the opposite side of the issue from the main character and is therefore not only the antagonist, but a very powerful and worthy antagonist. It would be possible to tell the story of *The Verdict* from Edward Concannon's point of view where Frank Galvin is the opposition—except for one thing. Frank Galvin is a down-and-out drunken, flat broke, failed attorney who's trying his last case. Concannon is the head of a respected legal firm with generous assets at its command.

The antagonist, whether overtly evil or merely opposed to the main character, is always more powerful and has more resources than the protagonist. If this were not the case, the main character would have no opposition in reaching the external goal and therefore there would be no dramatic conflict and no story to tell. No person or society would be changed by the main character's easy acquisition of the goal.

Scribble Exercise:

❏ In your screenplay, what external goal does the antagonist want?

❏ In your screenplay, what are the consequences if the antagonist does/does not reach that goal?

❏ In your screenplay, what is the antagonist's moral ethos, that is, his or her values?

❏ In your screenplay, how are the antagonist's values opposed to the values of the main character?

❏ In your screenplay, how are the antagonist's values opposed to the values of the audience *in the context of the story being told?*

PRACTICAL TECHNIQUES FOR DISCOVERING CHARACTER

The single most productive activity you can do to evoke character is to *listen*. Allow yourself to be the channel of communication for your characters. They will speak to you, through you, if you allow them to.

The most effective listening technique is to write a character study like the condensed example that follows in this chapter. The word "write" does not mean to *compose*, but rather to allow to be written. That is, put your fingers on the keyboard and wait. And listen. Listen and wait. Sooner or later your character will begin to talk, to tell stories, to relate personal history. When that starts happening, you start typing and you don't stop until the character has nothing more to say. Chances are you'll have somewhere between thirty to sixty pages of *stuff*.

Chances are also that none of this *stuff* will go into your screenplay. But remember, that's not what you were listening for. You were listening for the character's voice, for the surprises. You were getting past your own preconceptions and allowing the character to speak his or her own voice. There is no right or wrong to this process of bringing forth a character. No one except you will read it. In fact, when you're finished, the best thing you can do with the character study is to put it in a drawer and forget about it.

Well, to be honest, there are a couple of rules for writing character studies.

1. **Always write in present tense**. We are all used to writing in past tense because of reading novels and short stories, but screenplays happen now, and they are always written in present tense. Form the discipline of writing your character study in present tense to help your character *do* rather than *think* or *feel*. Remember that drama is *conflict* and characters are *action*.

59

2. Always write in active voice. Never say, "Trees can be seen from the window." Instead, "Trees are outside the window." This discipline also helps you when you write your screenplay to keep the action description alive and moving.

Scribble Exercise:

❏ Write a two- to four-page narrative in present tense, active voice, discussing the objects in your *main character's* living space. Let the character speak to you through the objects. By what *actions* did he or she acquire them? What *values* do the objects represent?

❏ Write a two- to four-page narrative in present tense, active voice, bringing your *main character* from some point in the past up to the point of the story's opening. What did he or she do just before coming on screen?

❏ Write a two- to four-page narrative in present tense, active voice, discussing the objects in your antagonist's living space. Let the character speak to you through the objects. By what *actions* did he or she acquire them? What *values* do the objects represent?

❏ Write a two- to four-page narrative in present tense, active voice, bringing your *antagonist* from some point in the past up to the point of the story's opening. What did he or she do just before coming on screen?

There's one more enlightening character exercise you might want to try. Find a friend who's willing to cooperate with you on a character discovery journey. Your friend is a lump of clay. The lump cannot ask questions and cannot reason or understand motivations. The lump can only do those physical activities you direct it to do. Your job is to direct the lump (your friend) to walk, sit, stand, and move like your character. Remember, you cannot provide motivations but only physical descriptions such as "turn your feet out," "bend your knees," hold your head erect," etc. You are creating a living sculpture of your main character.

The point of this sculpture exercise is not to find a physical description that you will put in your screenplay. In fact, you should never describe your characters physically, but rather metaphorically. Instead, the purpose of the exercise is to allow you to access your character through a different channel. You will be surprised to learn some things about your character that you did not know, and to be disabused of some things you thought you did know.

Now that you have a sense of your character's self-concept, values, and actions, spend the next two days being your character whenever you get the chance. Go to the grocery store or the gym or on a date as your character. If anyone says you're acting strangely, by the way, just tell them you're a writer.

SAMPLE CHARACTER STUDY

ALEXANDRA BARNARD

Alice Plucinski has no intention of trying out for the high school pep squad. She really goes along just to keep her friend Millie company. When the two of them step into the gym and see thirty other girls all practicing jumps and leaps and cheers that they've rehearsed for weeks just to get ready for this day, Alice is absolutely positive she doesn't want to have anything to do with it. She'll just sit on the stage and read and wait for Millie so they can walk home together.

It isn't that Alice has anything against joining the pep squad, it's just that she isn't meant to be there. In fact, Alice isn't meant to be anywhere—certainly not in Weybourne, Massachusetts, not with Karl and Helen Plucinski, not in Catholic Youth Council at 6:00 every Sunday night after having already been to Mass in the morning, not in Ralph Waldo Emerson High School, and never in the Stak-Rite Pasteboard Box Company where both her father and mother work, as does most everyone else in Weybourne.

There's no particular place Alice is meant to be, either now or when she is *grown up*. Grown up. That is what Alice is meant to be, and all of her life up till now has been a mistake, a huge miscalculation on somebody's part. She can never figure out just whose mistake it is, of course, because no matter how she tries to phrase the question, no one has a good answer. All Alice knows is that grown up means that if nobody gives you what you need, you can take it for yourself.

Several other girls walk back toward the stage shaking pom-poms and twirling batons. They all look very satisfied with themselves. One of the girls tosses her baton high in the air, then hops up with a perky, twisting jump to seat herself on the apron next to Alice and catch the falling, spinning baton behind her back without even looking at it.

64

Alice glances at the girl and her eyes fall on the baton lying on the stage between them. The girl smiles a condescending invitation, "Sure, go ahead and try it if you want."

Alice runs her long fingers over its rifled shaft. It doesn't feel the least bit awkward to her as she plaits each finger over the shaft and twists it into a slow, pulsating strobe of a circle. She leans forward off the stage for room enough to make the baton move faster, and before she knows it Alice is on the gym floor, her feet unconsciously repeating the same steps she's seen the line of girls practicing while she easily passes the twirling baton from one hand to the other.

Somewhere in the gym the recorded music stops. Alice doesn't. She's still keeping the beat, twirling and dancing with her eyes fixed on the flashing baton. Everyone in the gym is watching her. Her rhythm never falters until she slows the baton down to a stop. No one in the gymnasium says a word.

For one brief instant, Alice nearly joins the pep squad. Instead, she quietly replaces the baton on the stage apron, says thank you very politely to the startled girl, then turns her back and walks through the big double doors outside—and never looks back on Ralph Waldo Emerson High School or Weybourne, Massachusetts again.

With $128, one suitcase, and a first-place certificate in the district-wide typing tournament, Alice figures she has enough to get started. The first bus out of town that afternoon is going in the direction of New York and that's good enough for her. Within a month she's sharing a one-bedroom apartment with two other girls on West 22nd Street, and she's grabbed a job with the Hightower Literary Agency International, Ltd., where her typing skills win her the position of Associate Manuscript Editor.

Hightower takes column inch advertisements in the back pages of such literary lights as *Popular Mechanics* and the *New York Herald*

65

Tribune. For $86 a week, Alice sits at an ancient rolltop desk reading the multitude of hopeful manuscripts. She returns each submission with a copy of one or another form letter which compliments the author on insightful brilliance and ease of style while at the same time strongly suggesting that the writer could benefit enormously from the consultations of the Hightower senior staff who would be only too happy to provide instruction for the nominal tutorial fee of $50 per submission. At no extra charge, of course, the writer will be entitled to Hightower's tireless efforts at placing such quality writing in the finest journals available. Alice is not only the Associate Manuscript Editor, but also the senior staff—Harrison Matterlink, Carlyle Williams-Taylor, Jonelle Donalds, Gregory C. Engberg, etc., etc.— professional authors, journalists, and poets all. It's not easy keeping track of just which famous member of the Hightower senior staff has critiqued which manuscript, but Alice quickly works out an index card coding system which ensures that each of her responses is fresh, prompt, and, above all, encouraging if not laudatory. She becomes so skillful, in fact, at saying just the right thing to each hopeful, that the $50 checks keep arriving in the daily mail, and in her first year she sin-gle-handedly increases the Hightower business by 20 percent. It's training in poignant enticement she could get nowhere else.

From time to time, of course, a client will actually find his way to the Hightower offices in person, usually bearing a large, string-bound cardboard box containing his recent masterpiece which he would like to have placed with Doubleday by next week at the latest. Alice is always quick to point out that this is merely a branch office of Hightower, Ltd., and she will of course have to forward his opus to the head of literary development who, she hints, will be returning from London any day now. After fifteen minutes or so, the client usually leaves full of hope and promises, not to mention $50 lighter, and Alice makes a note on his index card to be sure to send a handwritten "sorry for the delay in our response to your very promising work" after six weeks or so. It's a seduction that she can practice freshly each day, and feel nothing for the hopefuls.

Late one July afternoon, however, a young man appears at Alice's desk carrying a slim binder of short stories. He is a dental student who likes to write in his spare time. He would appreciate Hightower's opinion. He hands her his check and is about to disappear when Alice finds herself volunteering to take a look at the stories while he waits. She's only an associate editor, she reminded him, but perhaps, if the stories are good, she could speed the process of acceptance. He thanks her, and quietly takes a seat on the wooden bus bench that serves as the agency's waiting room across from Alice's desk.

Perhaps it's his soft brown eyes, or the slight accent of his speech which Alice can't place, but she puts aside her other work and begins to read the young dental student's stories. Each one has a lulling, dreamlike quality that, in the end, is swiftly and skillfully betrayed in a jolt of unexpected reality, a knife blade slicing through a sleeper's eyeball. They're disturbing, at the same time captivating, and Alice has no idea what to do with them. She has no association with any legitimate agency, and the Hightower Literary Agency International, Ltd., certainly has no earthly way of selling the young author's material. It's late in the day and Alice decides it will be easier to disillusion the young author with food in his stomach, so she suggests that they talk about his work over a bite of dinner.

He is Raimundo Vargas, from Argentina. He is wealthy, and he has no desire whatsoever to become a dentist. That is his father's idea. But Raimundo passionately wants to be a writer. He has agreed with his father's plan to come to America to study, but only in order to be in the creative atmosphere of New York. He spends every evening after classes in Greenwich Village, frequenting several coffee houses where writers and artists gather to talk, complain, rail, and eat and drink whatever Raimundo is willing to pay for, which is, more often than not, everything. That evening, Alice meets a world she doesn't even know exists—actors, writers, painters—a fantastic, swirling world of creative ideas and half-baked notions, talent, and sham that makes her dizzy with possibility.

Alice moves in to live with Raimundo for two years. He never writes another story. He does manage to graduate from dental school and opens a practice on the west side which quickly becomes a thriving success. Alice returns to the Hightower Literary Agency International, Ltd., only once, to spend five minutes packing up the few personal things in her desk. She never explains the secrets of her index card coding system to anyone else in the office, which results in the Agency's profits for the next year falling considerably below expectations.

While Raimundo knuckles down to the critical years of his dental studies, Alice studies the energy of New York. She takes a job as a waitress in a coffee house so she can ask naive questions of the actors and dancers and singers to whose world she is attracted. She watches them play their parts at the table, watches them practice their steps on the streets, sing their songs in the restrooms, brag about their auditions, name names, and loudly give advice to each other. Alice soaks up every word.

On the day she shows up outside the Schubert Theatre in a long line of hopefuls trying out for the chorus in a new Broadway show, she's never had an acting, singing, or dancing lesson in her life, and she doesn't make it in the chorus. She gets a supporting role—thirteen lines, a dance solo, and a solid laugh on one exit when she deliberately slams her hips into a stony-faced butler to boot him away from the door. The show doesn't last a week, but Alice is now Alexandra Cantabella, after Raimundo's grandmother.

Alex's abbreviated Broadway career also produces an agent. As soon as the show closes she walks fifteen blocks straight into his office to ask what's up next. As it happens, he has an unfilled spot for a singer, three weeks on a cruise ship to the Caribbean. Alex snaps it up. She then walks to the nearest record store and buys a copy of every pop album she likes the looks of. For the next two weeks she listens to the stereo, soaking in the lyrics, inflections, and phrasing of each song into her eidetic memory until she has a repertoire of over fifty tunes ranging from the Big Band Era to the present. In the evening she traipses from one nightclub to another, standing in each only long enough to catch the female singer's act and make an indelible print of every movement and gesture. In one afternoon in the garment district she buys six evening gowns, three cocktail dresses, accessories, and two counterfeit Louis Vitton suitcases. By the time the cruise ship sails, Alex is twenty-one years old and a seasoned pro.

She's learned just enough Spanish from Raimundo to endear herself to the waiters, busboys, and bartenders on the ship. She jokes and laughs with them, drinks in their cabins at night, and, based on her experience as a waitress, lets it be known soon after coming aboard that she intends to share any tips she receives with the crew who work her show in the lounge. In return, they make it a point to speak to their tables in enthusiastic asides about an act the customers won't want to miss, and they mix the drinks a little stronger before Alex comes on stage. After the first week, there is a standing-room-only crowd each night of her performance.

Thanks to the faceless, earnest authors of Hightower, Alex's general knowledge, although sketchy and frequently in error, is broad enough to let her join into any conversation at the customers' tables, where she's often invited after doing her act; she can tell a good, entertaining story, and she seems to know instinctively how to say just what someone wants to hear. As a result, she is as popular off the stage as on, and quickly becomes the favorite of several men on the cruise.

One of these men is Morris Kaplan, a fifty-year-old restaurateur who owns a chain of eateries on the east coast. Kaplan is one of the first to recognize fast food as the trend in American dining, and also one of the first to realize that you have to sell a ton of pre-cooked hamburgers to turn the same profit as one chateaubriand and lobster bisque dinner for two. He quickly channels the revenues from his roadside successes into four-star dining establishments expensively located in selected cities. When the cruise ship returns to New York on its last weekend, Kaplan slips Alex his card and jovially invites her to come see him if she ever wants to get into the restaurant business.

Monday morning she's in Kaplan's office before he arrives. Kaplan starts her to work immediately as a hostess in his Manhattan flagship, and by that afternoon also puts her up in a mid-town apartment where he visits regularly one evening a week. By the time Morris Kaplan dies of a heart attack at fifty-five, Alex is running six Kaplan restaurants from New York to Atlanta. In her time, she hires and fires staff from French chefs to carpet cleaners, decorates in styles from Regency to Italian bistro, balances books, and develops the eye to spot a profit item from half a mile distant. By twenty-six years old, she is a pro at providing exactly what someone wants, and Weybourne, Massachusetts is all but forgotten.

Yet Alice Plucinski and Weybourne lurk somewhere deep inside Alex Cantabella so insidiously that she can never purge them completely. They taunt her never to stay in one place too long lest she be found out. Always keep moving on, or you might one day look up and discover you've never left.

She touches love only once. For six months after Morris's death, Alex continues with the Kaplan Corporation, but she knows her time is limited. With no clear idea of where to go next, she enrolls in C.C.N.Y. courses hoping that, if nothing else, they will provide her with some direction.

The class she enjoys most is American History, taught by a young instructor not much older than Alex herself. It is the time when revisionist history is popular on college campuses, and Philip Dermott is eager to debunk the national myths with which Alex and every other American have grown up. She finds to her delight that the Revolution and the settling of the continent had as much to do with personal gain as with highblown ideals about equality and freedom. It was, in fact, all about power, and that is something Alex can understand perfectly.

70

What she cannot understand so easily is Phil. They start seeing each other when Alex comes to him for help with one of her papers. Like all men, he is clearly impressed by her beauty, and Alex senses that somewhere underneath he is crying out for her to give him some sign that she also feels attracted to him. But Alex has never been genuinely, deeply attracted to anyone, so the feelings she has are as unfamiliar to her as the Byzantine workings of politics in government. It is some time before she admits that the stirrings inside her are, in truth, love. At first she mistakes them for an impressionable schoolgirl's infatuation with Phil's intellect, a quality which she has not encountered in other men who, although intelligent enough, used their intelligence only in the shrewd manipulation of those around them.

Phil is different. He is gentle, trusting, and, once she gets through the professional distance of the teacher's exterior, very caring about her as a person. He even invites her to help him with the research he's conducting for a book, yet there is nothing manipulative about his treatment of her. If anything, he seems to see her as an equal, if not in qualifications then at least in ability, and she throws herself into the project with more energy than she has ever before had to apply. For months they work side by side, researching, coding, transcribing, and sorting through mounds of data. Alex is thrilled every minute of it, aware more and more that the work itself provides only a small part of her enthusiasm. The real energy of her devotion, she admits to herself one evening while working late on a particularly difficult chapter, comes from being near Phil. She knows now that she is very much in love with him. From then on, the enthusiasm takes on an electric quality, a feeding back and forth which builds up an unbearable tension in both of them.

The tension explodes one night in a frenzy of tongue-tied confession, adulation, and passionate yearning which culminates in the two of them making love on the office floor. Afterwards they lie in each other's arms listening to the sounds of New York below while the janitors wax and polish the hallways outside, each wondering where to go

71

from here, and each not quite trusting the other not to betray something so precious.

In the end, Alex is the betrayer. Love is simply too big a risk to take. It strikes too close, demands of her a devotion which she is unable to give. She cannot, in fact, conceive of being her own person while at the same time feeling something for someone else. She has read what psychologists say about love, that the only clinical definition the science is able to offer is that love is a feeling beyond simply wanting to be with someone else, it is a drive to do things for that person before doing them for yourself. She has no doubt that Phil feels that way toward her, yet she cannot risk feeling that way toward him. She has other things to do, other places to go.

She quits before the semester ends and heads for Newport, Rhode Island. Dr. Daniel Barnard is there, a plastic surgeon whose wife does not understand him. Alex understands Dr. Barnard very well.

Scribble Exercise:

❑ What is Alex's self-concept? How does she see herself in the world, and how does she want the world to see her?

❑ What are Alex's values?

❑ What actress would you cast as Alex?

❑ Apart from commercial attraction, why would you cast this particular actress? What does this actress embody that conveys Alex's self-concept?

CHAPTER FIVE

SCREEN CONTEXT

"Screenwriters fashion more than plot and character. They create the substantive milieu and the moral climate that locate the story in a *cosmos of credibility*."

— Nick Tramontane

All right, now we have our screenplay structure building made of the essential dramatic building blocks that are held together by the mortar of character. Let's stretch the analogy a bit further and establish some landscaping to encompass and complement the building. Like any physical edifice in a neighborhood, a screenplay fits within a certain world. However, whereas a physical building simply exists within its community, a screenplay actually both creates and responds to the world that it lives in.

The idea of context for a screen story is one of the most difficult aspects of screenwriting to define. It is at one and the same time something the screenwriter creates, and yet something over which the screenwriter has no ultimate control. Because filmmaking is a collaborative art, there are hundreds of people from the cinematographer to the actors to the director who will contribute to the overall context of the film on screen. However, the screenwriter is the initial creator, and without the context fabricated on paper, none of the other contributors to the film have a *community* for the picture to live in.

COSMOS OF CREDIBILITY

When an audience enters the theater, they do so with what is called the *willing suspension of disbelief.* That is, they know that what they are about to see is not *real*. In fact, that's why they came to the movie, to see something that makes more sense than the real world, that provides in two hours a kind of paradigm for the way the world ought to be or could be. They came to laugh or cry or be outraged or made happy by events on screen that are somehow sharper and more comprehensible than the everyday world they live in. They recognize inherently that the illusion they've come to witness is one where actions and emotions are more articulate, more intense, than the ordinary. In truth, the world on the screen is a *hyper-reality*.

This quality of hyper-reality is one that distinguishes film from written literature and from other forms of drama. The basic aesthetic difference has to do with how our perceptions adjust to the dichotomy between imagination and reality.

The prose form of novels and short stories is often the least restricted medium for the imagination because the indistinct mental images created by words on a page aren't at all like the specific, definitive pictures in a film. Movies do not, in fact, deal well with fantasy. Of course, they can transport us to a fantasy realm, but once we are there, that realm takes on an aesthetically concrete form. Have you ever been unsettled and disappointed by the filmed version of a favorite novel? Of course, because the illusory picture you created in your head of the world of the novel was insubstantial. You conjured up images of the characters and settings that seemed complete, and yet were actually only vague connect-the-dots portraits with great amounts of detail missing. But a movie made out of your novel presents you with somebody else's visual representation of what you had in your mind's eye. In the film, you can count the buttons on the actor's shirt, and there is no way the concrete likeness of film can ever agree with the fickle notions inside your head. The aesthetic perceptions are simply not the same at all.

Of course, a really good movie can involve us to the extent that we completely forget the outside world for a couple of hours precisely because of our total immersion in the specific hyper-reality of the movie.

76

A stage play, on the other hand, will always be unreal, no matter how naturalistic the sets, costumes, etc. Watching live theater is something like looking through a transparent wall. It is our voyeuristic insight into the lives of characters who live on the other side. Yet, no matter how engaging the play may be, our peripheral consciousness is always aware that we have deliberately, willingly isolated the stage from the outside world. In movies, though, we are hurled through the aesthetic wall to actually live and get shot at and scream and laugh and be joyful and frightened neck-and-neck with the characters on the screen in a concentrated dose of intense reality.

So, when the audience enters the movie theater, the *willing suspension of disbelief* becomes, in effect, a contract. The audience says implicitly to the filmmakers, "we will enthusiastically enter your special world of hyper-reality as long *as you don't break the rules* and step outside of the bounds of the Cosmos of Credibility."

Rules? Remember that the screenwriter has compressed the time and selected the events of the drama. That means the screenwriter has already established rules by setting up a particular, artificial context, and now must be very skillful in maintaining the Cosmos of Credibility generated by that context. The paradox is that while the audience wants to have the experience of the hyper-reality, they are continually asking questions based on their sense of how everyday authentic reality works. In other words, the screenwriter has to sell the hyper-reality to the audience in such a way that they never have the opportunity to ask, "But why don't the characters just...?".

If the audience ever asks the *"But why don't they just...?"* question without receiving a context-appropriate answer, the implicit contract of trust in the filmmakers is broken. The Cosmos of Credibility is violated, and the audience will never be able to completely reenter the special world of the movie.

But what can the frail screenwriter do to ensure that the context of the film will not be violated by the hundreds of other dominant crew members who will work on the film? There are no guarantees, of course, but a good screenwriter is, first and foremost, a meticulous, demanding artisan. Remember, it's your job to *make the story work*. You must always ask yourself the same questions your audience will ask of the film, the hundreds of "What if?" and "Why not?" and "How did we get here?" inquiries that must be satisfied before the audience even has a chance to ask them.

Scribble Exercise:

❑ What movie adaptations have you seen that disappointed you after having read the novel? How did these films violate the context in ways that didn't fit your mind's eye vision of the characters and story?

❑ Did the following films meet your mind's eye expectations of context based on your reading of the novel?

The Godfather (I and II)

The Firm

Silence of the Lambs

❑ What films have you seen adapted from stage plays that worked well? What films were disappointing? Why?

❏ Did the following films meet your mind's eye expectations of context based on your experience of the stage play?

Driving Miss Daisy (Directed by Bruce Beresford, with Morgan Freeman and Jessica Tandy, 1989)

The Glass Menagerie (Directed by Paul Newman, with John Malkovich and Joanne Woodward, 1987)

Romeo and Juliet (Directed by Franco Zefferelli, 1968)

Hamlet (Kenneth Branagh, 1996; Mel Gibson, 1990; Lawrence Olivier, 1948?)

RESEARCH AND INVESTIGATION

The screenwriter must become the world's leading authority on the particular context you create for the script. In some cases this means going to the library and doing research; in other cases it may mean visiting an actual location where your story occurs, or interviewing people who are familiar with the kinds of events you are writing about. You may, for instance, need to interview your local police to find out how they handle particular procedures. There is a wealth of information now on the Internet, and hundreds of willing experts who will gladly help you with background information for your screenplay. With just a little bit of digging, you should be able to find out virtually anything you need to know about a particular subject.

However, while you're gathering facts, don't forget to gather *feelings*. Read novels written in the genre you are attempting, especially the masters of the medium. If you intend to write a private detective story, for example, you should read Raymond Chandler, Dashiell Hammett, and some of their contemporary successors in order to get a feel for the language of the characters and their environment. You don't need to imitate these writers, you simply need to absorb the context they've created. Learn to live on that shadowy side of the street so that your vision is carried into your screenplay.

"I find television very educating. Every time somebody turns on the set, I go into the other room and read a book."
— Groucho Marx

Of course, you need to watch all the films you can that deal with stories or contexts that are similar to yours. Did the films work or not? What mistakes in context were made? If they were successful, what elements made them successful?

81

Now, before you begin writing, take all the research you've collected—and forget it. Put it in an envelope and lock it in a drawer. Your job is not to relate a factual documentary, but to tell a story. Very often writers become enamored of their research and let it overwhelm them. They try to wedge in all the fascinating tidbits of information, and thereby squeeze the life out of the story they're trying to tell. Soak up the minutiae of your research, then ignore it. Don't let facts get in the way of truth.

WHAT *ARE* YOU DOING?

To be honest, the next step in creating context isn't writing as most people think of the craft, but it is nonetheless an essential part of the creation or context. Let's call this phase *couch writing*. It's the time you spend lying back on the sofa or loafing under a tree in the park and letting your imagination hover and spiral and make magical correlations for your story. However, although couch writing may be free-floating in the universe, it is not completely without direction. It isn't an excuse to do nothing. Instead, you are using what is now referred to as fuzzy logic to make specific kinds of associations that have to do with your story's context. If you find yourself thinking about what to buy Uncle Fred for his birthday, that's okay, but bring yourself back to musing about the particular story you want to tell. The free-form part is that you needn't think about your story in any particularly linear fashion. Instead, you must steep your creative self in the time and place and random events of your story. Listen to music, look at photographs, and, above all, jot down random notes of your impressions. Not everything will wind up in your screenplay, of course, but you'll be surprised how much of your effervescent daydreaming will produce events, characters, and snatches of dialogue that contribute to the Cosmos of Credibility.

Again, in the same way that you want to allow your characters to emerge rather than fabricating them, you want to allow the context to speak for its own genuineness without trying to mangle it into shape.

82

ELEMENTS OF CONTEXT

Here's the paradox, however. It is one thing to say that writing is all free-form imagination, and something entirely different to produce a screenplay that someone else wants to read. Good screenwriting is extraordinarily hard work. It is not merely spontaneous musing, but carefully crafted, well-thought-out literature. Good screenwriting obeys rules and has structure. You cannot produce a good screenplay by couch writing alone. You must take the raw input of your imagination and shape it into something that the public can grasp, something that sends an audience out of the theater satisfied that they have spent their time and their money well.

With regard to context, it is at one and the same time a crucial part of the film that the screenwriter creates, and yet a component over which the screenwriter has no ultimate control. It is, therefore, almost impossible to lay down any kind of codex for successfully establishing context in your screenplay. Given that caveat, however, let's look at several essential context elements the screenwriter should be alert to.

1. **Dramatic Emphasis**. What is the emotional hook that ties the audience to the story? What does the audience *care* about? It is sometimes easy when we are writing to lose track of the thing that keeps the audience in their seats, the very simple emotional identification with the plight of the main character. At its simplest, this emotional hook is the audience's desire for the main character to reach the worthy external goal. Imagine a thriller story, for instance, where the character's external goal is to stay alive. That is a potent emotional hook for the audience, and every event that deviates from that dramatic emphasis diminishes the audience's connection to the story. Every scene the writer spends indulging an enthusiasm for historical fact or social commentary will mutilate the audience's umbilical connection to the main character. The screenwriter must never forget why the *audience* is watching the movie.

83

2. **Physical World**. As we will discuss Chapter Seven on style, it is not up to the screenwriter to literally describe the physical world of the story. In fact, the less explicit physical description in a screenplay the better. However, a screenwriter is concerned with the metaphorical expression of the physical world and, more specifically, the reasonable expectations of place and artifact. By compressing time and selecting events, the screenwriter has also limited the physical world in which the story occurs, and must be aware of the audience's beliefs about that world. It would be preposterous, of course, for the women of *Sense and Sensibility* to catch the subway into London. And yet, errors of nearly equal, even if not so obvious, absurdity are made in films all the time. It is not that artifacts and places must be absolutely, invariably accurate in every detail, but that they must not disturb the audience's confidence. To do so is, at best, to violate the contract of trust in the willing suspension of disbelief, and at worst to completely jump into a different context.

3. **Time**. There are two kinds of time the screenwriter must be aware of: the ostensible *chronological time* in which the story occurs, and the *encompassing era* of the story. The apparent elapsed time is the audience's sense of how long it takes for the story to unfold. As we will examine in the next chapter, different genres of film generally occur in distinct spans of perceived time, even though all of them transpire in more or less two hours of real time. More crucial to the context for the screenwriter is the encompassing era for the story. There is always a treachery of time that is distant from that which we experience every day. Ironically, the further removed from our familiar time and place a story is, the less freedom the screenwriter has because it becomes increasingly difficult to create a credible context. It is essential, then, when dealing with removed time that you establish clearly marked pathways for the audience to follow. Science fiction raises par-

ticularly difficult issues of time, for example. Moving far into the future or far into space necessarily presupposes that we are in a vastly different social system as well as technology. To keep the audience firmly located, the writer must establish the rules of that social system very, very quickly, yet unlike written literature, filmed science fiction does not have the liberty to explain the idiosyncrasies. The audience must understand them by example more or less instantly. In other words, just because you are dealing with a story in the past or the future does not mean that you are free to do anything you'd like. In fact, you are more restricted because the audience can so easily become confused about where they are and how they got there.

As you write, imagine that you are leading a group of children on a journey through the forest at night. No matter how much they may want the excitement of the adventure, they have abandoned the safety and comfort of their homes, and they very much need to trust that you will take care of them, that you won't let them get lost in the forest.

4. Character Ethos. We've discussed character as an element of dramatic screenwriting, but character is also a function of context, that is, the characters live in a particular time and place, and their attitudes, behaviors, and values are established by and resonate in the milieu they inhabit.

The most obvious impression we get of this interdependence of character and context is in the language the characters use. Characters need to speak in a simulacrum of the language of time they represent, and yet this is clearly not always possible. To have William Wallace and the other characters of *Braveheart* speaking accurate thirteenth-century Scots dialect would clearly be incomprehensible to the audience. Yet, to have them speaking modern-day vernacular would be equally jarring, so screenwriter Randall Wallace had to develop a rhythmic structure that implied a historical time without trying to duplicate it literally.

Language, though, is an expression of attitude, of values, and in this area, context and character become more difficult to manage. To some extent because movie stars embody certain attitudes regardless of the character they play, and to some extent because the commercial demands of the motion picture industry make accuracy an easily sacrificed quantity, many films pay less attention to this aspect of character-context than they should. The result is that we get a jumble of styles and attitudes in a picture such as *Robin Hood: Prince of Thieves* where there is no consistency of portrayal among the various characters, and consequently absolutely no integrity of context.

In the best of circumstances, the screenwriter will be able to create characters that exist naturally within their context, and those characters' values and behaviors will be determined only by the context in which they live, rather than by an imposed contemporary moral or behavioral standard that bears no relationship to the time being portrayed.

Scribble Exercise:

Write a context study that explores and identifies the principal elements of dramatic emphasis, place, time, and character ethos in your screenplay. There's no right or wrong way to do the context exercise except that, as in the character study, you should form the discipline of writing in present tense, active voice.

❏ What is the primary emotional hook of your story?

❏ What are the audience's expectations of place and artifact for your story?

❏ How does your story create credibility within the dramatic compression of time without violating the audience's willing suspension of disbelief?

❏ What are the general attitudes and values and behaviors of your characters that are established by the time and place in which they live?

87

CHAPTER SIX

SCREEN GENRES

"Nothing leads so straight to futility as literary ambitions without systematic knowledge."

— H.G. Wells

EXPECTATIONS OF FORM

Originally a French word meaning *gender*, *genre* has come to describe certain styles of drama, painting, literature, film, and other arts that are characterized by a particular form or content. We often speak of "genre fiction" or "genre film," especially when discussing something like the horror novels of Stephen King or the *film noir* detective movies of the 1940s, but for the most part there are no universally agreed-upon definitions that distinguish one unique style from another. Nevertheless, it can be helpful to use the concept of genre to sort out different types of movies and to determine what context elements are common to each. However, keep in mind that the divisions between genres on the following chart are arbitrary for the purpose of this discussion. Think of the boundaries between genres as semi-permeable membranes rather than fortress walls.

Continuum of Screen Genres

Drama is the narrative of a *significant transition* in the life of a character and therefore in a society.

➡ **Increasing Personal Jeopardy Equals Increasing Societal Consequence ➡**

	Willingness to Become Fully Alive					**Willingness to Live**			**Willingness to Die**	
	Intrapersonal Anguish	Interpersonal Conflict	Comedy	Fairy Tale	Personal Quest	Detective	Horror	Thriller	Action-Adventure	Metaphysical Anguish
	Many European films; early Ingmar Bergman films	Ordinary People; Terms of Endearment; Tender Mercies, etc.	The Birdcage; Priscilla Queen of the Desert; A Fish Called Wanda, etc.	Pretty Woman; The Piano; Sense and Sensibility; Good Will Hunting; Titanic, etc.	Chariots of Fire; Dead Man Walking; Quiz Show; Larry Flynn, etc.	Seven; The Maltese Falcon; Chinatown; The Usual Suspects; Silence of the Lambs, etc.	Poltergeist; Frankenstein; Dracula; Friday the 13th; Halloween, etc.	North by Northwest; Three Days of the Condor; Alien; Breakdown, etc.	Braveheart; Con Air; Star Wars; The Guns of Navarone; ID4; all Westerns and War movies, etc.	Crimes and Misdemeanors; Amadeus, etc.

1. **Intrapersonal Anguish Genre** — Many European films, including the films of Ingmar Bergman, such as *Cries and Whispers*.

  ✓ **Dramatic Emphasis** tends to be about characters' self-revelation through the expiation of guilt or imagined guilt. There is very little action. Instead, these films are largely built on dialogue scenes interspersed with long stretches of carefully photographed but essentially static images designed to have the audience imagine what is occurring inside the characters. They often use literary devices such as voice-over narratives and flashback scenes to gain access to the characters' interiors.

  ✓ **Physical World** is often confined, cluttered, a musty counterpart of the internal self. Objects such as mirrors or windows frequently have a symbolic or emblematic value intended to represent a character's inexpressible anguish of self-discovery.

  ✓ **Time** is fairly short, generally over a night or a weekend that is the culmination of a lifetime of distress.

  ✓ **Character Ethos** involves people who are existential, tormented by their own self-doubts, and unyielding in their psychological stasis.

2. **Interpersonal Conflict Genre** — *Ordinary People, Terms of Endearment, Tender Mercies, Steel Magnolias, Marvin's Room*.

  ✓ **Dramatic Emphasis** is on the *passion* the characters employ to resolve or restore a relationship, usually with an estranged family member. There is frequently an emotionally charged event such as a wedding, funeral, or illness which brings disaffected family members together and sets the scene for reopening old wounds, thereby resolving hurts and misunderstandings.

91

✓ **Physical World** is customarily boxlike, limited, and inescapable. The characters are thrown together in a setting that mirrors their psychological predicament. Interpersonal Conflict films are often made from material that originally appeared as stage dramas occurring in one room or primarily one room, and while the films make an effort to expand into the world at large, the essential action of the drama usually does not require that the characters move out of their limited space, and, in fact, too much "air" in the setting may damage the intensity of the forced confrontation. If characters can escape the conflict, they will do so, whereas if they are forced to be physically in close proximity they are more likely to battle out their differences.

✓ **Time**, like the Intrapersonal Conflict drama, is fairly short, generally over a weekend or a couple of days because the sheer intensity of the emotions demands that the characters resolve their conflicts relatively quickly.

✓ **Character Ethos** involves characters who are frail, vulnerable, dimensional. These are perhaps the most true-to-life characters of movies.

3. Comedy Genre — *Modern Times, The General, Bringing Up Baby, La Cage aux Folles, Tootsie, As Good As It Gets.*

✓ **Dramatic Emphasis** is on the complete bafflement, shock, and surprise the characters encounter. Comedies are about adults acting like children, fascinated and bewildered by the world, but afraid to deal with it head-on. If comedy characters acted like adults, stopping to reason out their dilemma or to explain themselves in some sensible way, there would be no comedy. In the course of the comedy, especially comedy love stories, the characters grow from children to adolescents who manage to deal with their puzzling world in a more rational if not altogether completely adult manner.

✓ **Physical World** is unfamiliar, intimidating, exaggerated, and filled with slick, oily things that are hard to grasp, and footing that is precariously slippery. The world is a giant banana peel just waiting to skid out from under the characters' feet. Machinery, transportation, and social norms are as intimidating and unfathomable as the sensible people who are in charge of the world.

✓ **Time** is fairly short because of the exaggeration of the story. It is intense and frenetic, but the audience recognizes that the unreality of comedy cannot exist forever. There must be a conclusion where the comedy characters and situation are brought back into the real world.

✓ **Character Ethos** is the most open-ended and least harshly judged of any dramatic form. The nihilistic characters of comedy can get away with virtually anything in their riotous, unrestrained world, and can even defy natural laws of time and space in ways that would break the rules of context for an audience in a different genre of film.

4. **Fairy Tale** — *Pretty Woman, The Piano, Sense and Sensibility, Good Will Hunting, Titanic.*

✓ **Dramatic Emphasis** is on release from bondage. The main character is an emotional captive to other characters, frequently the family, and must discover the means of liberation.

✓ **The Physical World** is confining — a sinking ship, a rural hamlet, a primitive island — and as restrictive as the character's emotional or spiritual world. There is often a physical object or action which serves as a symbolic key to the emancipation, such as the piano, the wedding dress, or the dance.

✓ **Time** is most often controlled by the characters and the setting. Although there may be an external clock such as the

93

sinking ship, usually the characters themselves determine the time span during which their actions occur by choosing to act or not act.

✓ **Character Ethos** is very sharply defined good and bad. Characters are emblematic rather than dimensional. There is normally a "fairy godmother" character who provides the secret for escape and is opposite lover for the main character.

5. Personal Quest — *Quiz Show, Chariots of Fire, Dead Man Walking, The People vs. Larry Flynt, The Shawshank Redemption.*

✓ **Dramatic Emphasis** is on achieving a personal quality such as integrity or honesty. This is an extremely difficult genre to write well because the notion of a personal quality is largely interior and screenwriters can easily fall into the trap of creating an Intrapersonal Anguish film instead. There must be a dramatic situation which commands emotional conflict with other characters and forces the main character to take *actions* that resonate with the personal quest, not merely scenes of the character brooding about despondently trying to come to grips with the internal need.

✓ **Physical World**, like that of the Intrapersonal Anguish genre, tends to be constrained. However, whereas the characters in the Intrapersonal Anguish dramas have elected their environments, the characters of the Personal Quest genre have somehow been put in a confined location, such as a prison or hospital, or in a position that is exactingly managed and disciplined by others, such as a sports team, the military, or a corporate office.

✓ **Time** is often quite long, perhaps months, although perceived time will appear to be short because the external goal or an extreme event will always loom as the consummate trial for the main character's integrity.

✓ **Character Ethos** is about the search for truth, an equivocal virtue versus moral certitude. The main character's intent is not so much to expiate guilt as to discover what the significance of guilt is, to determine what integrity consists of, and thereby to understand deficiency.

6. **Detective Genre** — *Chinatown, The Maltese Falcon, The Usual Suspects, Seven, The Silence of the Lambs.*

✓ **Dramatic Emphasis** is about the restoration of equilibrium. It is not about defeating all evil for all time, or even about justice, but about the righting of wrong. Society has developed a malignant aneurysm. It is a polluted, distasteful business dealing with the back side of civilization, but the detective seeks to clamp the abscess into place before it bursts into the world at large and infects us all.

✓ **Physical World** is an urban jungle filled with decay and the rotten detritus that the world outside of the shadows would rather not know about.

✓ **Time** is blurred, neither day nor night, and as vaporously shrouded as an intoxicated stupor.

✓ **Character Ethos** is about the thinking process. The detective is a character of wits rather than physical strength, a grey knight who walks the shady side of the street, yet possesses an inviolable code of honor, a seeker of truth in a world gone awry.

7. **Horror Genre** — *Frankenstein, Dracula, Friday the 13th, Halloween, Poltergeist, Invasion of the Body Snatchers.*

✓ **Dramatic Emphasis** is on raw fear, the terror of a supernatural monster that has absolute power over its human victims.

95

✓ **Physical World** is distorted, a maze of corridors and unknown recesses where the monster can hide, a world isolated from any outside help.

✓ **Time** is very short, usually twenty-four hours or less, because the audience instinctively recognizes that no one remains realistically isolated for a long period of time, and because the action is at such an intensity it cannot be sustained over a long time span.

✓ **Character Ethos** involves vulnerable but resourceful *everyman* characters who act out our fears in battling the overt evil of an inhuman monster, or the camouflaged evil of a monster that is masquerading as human.

8. Thriller Genre — *Three Days of the Condor, North by Northwest, Alien, Breakdown, Single White Female.*

✓ **Dramatic Emphasis** is on the main character's *willingness to stay alive.* There is an intense emotional identification with a life-or-death battle where the audience explores its own fears by experiencing those of the main character.

✓ **Physical World** is isolated from help and, as in the horror genre, made of a maze of corridors and unknown recesses. It is an expressionistic extension of the internal fears of the main character.

✓ **Time** is extremely short, normally twenty-four hours or less, because of the inherent incredibility of long-term isolation from outside help.

✓ **Character Ethos** involves a relative innocent who is drawn into a larger intrigue, but who discovers that the only way to remain alive is through self-reliance, taking charge and exposing the corruption to light. It is an expression of moral decay where the main character is caught up in a desperate situation that reveals a malevolent evil which, without the intrusion of the main character, will assault the larger community.

9. Action-Adventure Genre — all Westerns, war movies cops-and-robbers films, *Braveheart, Star Wars, Independence Day, The Guns of Navarone, Con Air, Saving Private Ryan.*

✓ **Dramatic Emphasis** is on the character's *willingness to die* for an idea, code, value, or supporting society.

✓ **Physical World** is a rousing environment, that is, one which is out of the ordinary, even exaggerated, the most hyper-real of the genres. It is a *masculine* world with room to maneuver and take physical action in the defense of a fragile or threatened civilization. Overall action takes place in a chase or a state of siege.

✓ **Time** can be fairly long, weeks or months, leading up to a climactic battle.

✓ **Character Ethos** involves an expression of high moral order where characters who are willing to die for an idea, code, society, or value go up against equally motivated antagonists who are *morally different* in a showdown battle of truth. Action-Adventure characters are larger than life and twice as grand. They are what we would be if only we could.

10. Metaphysical Anguish Genre — *Crimes and Misdemeanors, Amadeus.*

✓ **Dramatic Emphasis** is on the main character's risk of the immortal soul.

✓ **Physical World** is sophisticated, usually surrounded by the trappings of power and position.

97

✓ **Time** may be long while the main character slowly comes to realize that the battle is against God.

✓ **Character Ethos** involves an intelligent, resourceful, but morally untested character who battles to exert his or her self-concept over that of an irrational God.

These are very brief, thumbnail sketches of several genres, each of which would require a separate book to fully illustrate. They are offered here not as a construct for film criticism, but as a tool to help you understand the screenplay you want to write. Of course you will be able to find exceptions and objections to virtually every one of the categories, but take them as general tendencies and you'll find this a helpful map for navigating the treacherous waters of screenwriting. Some elements can clearly be used in more than one genre, but many are specific to a particular genre and cannot be mixed with others. For instance, the kind of main character who exists in an Action-Adventure story simply will not function in a Thriller. Although the two forms may exchange some life forces, they are fundamentally different genres.

You will also notice that the chart is a continuum. As personal jeopardy for the main character increases, so does the threat to the surrounding society. There is virtually nothing at stake for the surrounding society in an Intrapersonal Anguish film, which by its nature is about the internal workings of one character. The surrounding society in an Interpersonal Conflict story is probably no larger than the immediate family. However, what is at stake in an Action-Adventure is the security of a community or even the raw existence of a civilization, and that survival depends ultimately on one main character's willingness to die for the protection of that society.

Scribble Exercise:

❏ Where does your screenplay fit in the genre chart?

❏ If you think your screenplay does not fit one of these genres, what genre do you believe better describes the movie you want to write?

❏ What is your definition of that genre using the context elements discussed?

❏ Where does your new genre fit in the continuum of increasing personal and societal jeopardy?

CHAPTER SEVEN

SCREENWRITING STYLE

"Sometimes a Thing which seems very Thingish inside you is quite different when it gets out into the open and has other people looking at it."

— Winnie the Pooh in *The House at Pooh Corner*,
by A. A. Milne

No one curls up at night with a good screenplay. Even the best screenplay is an arduous document to read. Screenplays demand a greater degree of participatory imagination from the reader than practically any other form of literature except, perhaps, poetry. In fact, the best screenplays have more in common with verse than with novels or short stories or even other forms of dramatic writing. Good screenplays are evocative like poetry rather than descriptive like novels. They are rhythmic librettos waiting for the music of celluloid. They are narrative odes and epics.

The prevailing declaration about screenplays in Hollywood is that *The script is the blueprint*! meaning, presumably, that nothing can be built without the design specifications set forth in this hundred-plus page document. Of course, after the film is finished the same touts will shrug, *Well, the script is only a blueprint.*

The fact is that a script is far more than a sketch or outline for a motion picture. There is a famous, although perhaps apocryphal, story about Robert Riskin, the screenwriter for *It Happened One Night*, *Meet John Doe*, and many of the pictures directed by Frank Capra, who finally got fed up with all the talk about the whimsical "Capra touch." One day Riskin stalked into Capra's office, dropped 120 blank pieces of paper on the director's desk and declared, "Here, Frank, put the Capra touch on *that*."

Authentic or not, the story is illustrative of a fundamental truth — the screenwriter is the only member of the collaborative filmmaking team who creates something out of nothing. The fact is, everyone else who works on a movie interprets what the screenwriter created. The screenwriter is the only legitimate originator of a movie, and that means you have a unique responsibility to those who will come after you.

✓ You must keep in mind that words are the only tools of your trade. Film may be a visual medium (actually it's more than visual), but screenwriting is strictly limited to words on paper. You can't paste up photographs or submit sound recordings or explain what you meant later. What exists on the written page is the sole product of your craft and your art. That's it. That's all of it. Period.

✓ You are not the only person making the film. You probably will not be the director, and even if you are, there will be things that happen in the filmmaking process that you as a writer have no way of anticipating. This means that you do not direct the film on the page. You write cause-and-effect for action, characters, and to some extent settings — all the things we've talked about up until now. But you do not describe in detail where the actor stands or exactly how to read a line of dialogue, or precisely what selection of music must be used. To put it simply, screenwriters write in *images*, not pictures. Screenwriters write evocatively, not descriptively.

✓ You are an artisan. You owe the people who will interpret your script the most conscientiously crafted professional work you can turn out.

This last consideration has to do with the purely pragmatic aspect of formatting a screenplay, which often intimidates many beginning screenwriters. The most important consideration to keep in mind about screenplay format is, no matter what else you may hear or read, *there is no single, correct, always perfect screenplay format.* If it looks like a screenplay and reads like a screenplay, it's a screenplay.

However, having relieved you of that anxiety, let's look at the ways you can use the established conventions and devices of screenwriting to best tell a movie story on paper.

THE PRACTICAL — GUIDING THE READER'S EYE

The first screenplay you ever saw probably made your head swim with all those abbreviations and capitalization and indentations and strange margin settings. How in the world does anybody read this stuff? Good question. The fact is, screenplays are hard to read. They are part diagram and part literature, but the best of them are genuinely forms of poetry, and just like sonnets or haiku, these poems obey some rules of form and structure that help contain the story they have to tell.

Many of the peculiar characteristics of screenplay formatting are anachronistic holdovers from earlier days of the studio system when screenwriters produced *shooting scripts*, that is, scripts that were actually used to budget the films and develop production schedules. With computer graphics, miniaturized equipment, sophisticated lighting rigs, and a host of other state-of-the-art filmmaking techniques, it really isn't strictly necessary, for instance, to indicate whether a scene takes place INTerior or EXTerior the way it might have been thirty or fifty years ago. However, many of the conventions of screenwriting have remained as a kind of shorthand language that is understood within the industry. In fact, insightful use of this jargon can help you tell your story simply and directly.

The fact is, you are not writing and never will write a shooting script. You are writing a *selling script*. Do not clutter your presentation with useless abbreviations, numbers, and other indications that have nothing to do with telling the story. That is the test. Whenever you're tempted to add some adornment you've seen on a script, ask yourself if this bit of garnish actually helps you tell the story, or does it get in the way? Does it help the reader understand, or does it create noise on the page? Have you added mishmash to the page, or made the script read more smoothly?

The most fundamental law of screenplay format is: *Make the script easy to read*! You do not want your reader to have to work any harder than necessary. In fact, you don't want your reader to work at all, but to ecstatically flip through the pages of your script as if the movie were playing on the screen. This means that you don't want to interrupt the flow of the story with a lot of meaningless ornamental detail or authorial attempts to control the film. You want to manipulate the reader, not the movie. You want to move the reader's eye over the page in such a way that the characters and action are indelibly imprinted. You never want the reader to get lost on the page, to have to flip to prior pages to figure out how this scene got here or when a particular character entered.

Screenplay Formatting at its Simplest

1. Left margin: 1.5 inches
2. Right margin: 1.25 inches
3. Top & bottom: 1 inch
4. Tabs: starting from the "0" mark on your ruler, set tabs at:
   - Dialogue: 2.60 inches
   - Parentheticals: 3.25 inches
   - Character names: 4.0 inches
   - Transitionals (DISSOLVE TO): 7.0 inches, flush right

You want your script to be inviting to read. At the very least, that means type it well.

✓ Make your screenplay look neat and professional. Leave plenty of white space so that the page is easy on the eye. Keep a minimum of a one-inch margin all around the page. Paragraph frequently. Make it easy to read.

✓ Industry standard is Courier 12 type. Never use script or proportionately spaced type.

✓ Use only plain, white, 8-1/2 x 11 inch, 20-pound stock paper. Print on only one side of the page. Never use lined, colored, embossed, erasable, onionskin, or spiral-bound paper.

✓ Do not make corrections in ink, pencil, or Liquid Paper on the submission copy.

✓ Likewise, do not draw happy faces, arrows, or other marginalia on the pages trying to explain to the reader that a certain sentence or word should be placed somewhere else.

✓ Always check, double-check, and triple-check your spelling and punctuation. It does matter.

✓ Put the page numbers followed by a period in the upper right corners.

One of the silliest controversies to arise in recent years is the question of how a script should be bound. Traditionally scripts have been bound in plain card-stock covers and secured with brass brads. It is of no consequence whatever whether you use two brass brads or three. No one is going to refuse to read your script because of the number of brads holding it together. At the same time, keep your binding simple and unobtrusive. Do not use spiral bindings, book bindings, red satin ribbon, or any other fancy method of securing the pages, and never try to attract attention with hand-tooled leather covers, or gaudy, fluorescent colors.

Of course, you should always include a title page. Center the title of your script in all caps about one-third to one-half of the way down the page, then center "written by" or simply "by" directly below that, then your name centered directly below that — and be sure to include your own or your representative's address and telephone number with area code in the lower right corner of the page. In the lower left corner, type the copyright symbol (©), the year, and your name (see Chapter Nine for more on copyrights). Do not include draft numbers or completion dates. Remember, this is a *selling script*. No one needs to know when you wrote it.

Sample Title Page

George and Martha on the Planet Zylott

by

Your Name

Your Address or
Representative's
Name & Address
City, State   Zip
(Area Code) Phone
(Area Code)   Fax

I never write shot descriptions. Never say "We pull in" or "We see." How presumptuous to say that sort of thing. The only useful thing about the screenplay form is to tell you whether it's day or night, inside or outside. Everything else should be like a novel — clean and sharp and interesting to read.

— John Milius writer of *Apocalypse Now, Clear and Present Danger, The Wind and the Lion*, etc.

All right, you may or may not strictly agree with John Milius's assessment of the screenplay form, but let's accept his general thesis that a screenplay should be "clean and sharp and interesting to read." Certainly that prerequisite should be made of all writing—business, legal, medical, academic and whatnot—but it should unquestionably be true of writing that is meant to entertain.

Before we can explore the tangled paths of screenplay format, however, we need to understand what a scene is. The working definitions of scene can be quite different, and sometimes rather technical, depending on who is using the term. To a cinematographer, for instance, a scene refers to each separate camera setup where the angle of the shot must be changed and the lights have to be reset accordingly. Even the simplest scene of two people talking to each other requires at least three camera setups: a shot of person A, a shot of person B, and a shot of both A and B. Later these three separate strips of film, or scenes, will be cut together by the editor into one continuous scene which may, in fact, only be part of a larger scene. In the same sense, directors sometimes refer to scenes as dialogue exchanges or "moments" between characters, or even as the individual components of a complicated stunt. Screenwriters, however, always write in *master scenes*, that is, dramatic episodes that have a continuity of thought and action, but which may involve numerous characters and possibly even different locations.

Imagine a simple master scene. George and Martha are having an argument in their living room. The scene is set as

```
INT. GEORGE AND MARTHA'S HOUSE
George and Martha's tumultuous argument fills the
house.
```

Assuming we've met the characters of George and Martha earlier in the screenplay, this is all we need to know about the current action. Now suppose that in the course of their argument, Martha stalks off down the hallway into the bedroom, slams the door, and locks George out. George bangs on the door, then hurries outside to the bedroom patio glass door, but that's locked as well. He returns to the hallway and stands outside the bedroom door shouting at his wife while Martha is inside throwing clothes into a suitcase.

There are at least four locations involved in this scene: the living room, the hallway, the bedroom, and the outdoor patio. Each location requires a separate camera setup and the director will probably want to shoot each location from both characters' perspectives to allow as much choice as possible later in the editing room. However, for the screenwriter this is *one master scene with continuity of thought and action*. There is no need to identify each separate location with INT. or EXT. They all take place within the master location of George and Martha's house. Furthermore, you want the argument to be the primary dramatic ingredient of the scene, not the technical details of how the argument is portrayed. It's up to the director to decide the exact visual realization of this scene, but it's the screenwriter's responsibility to create a scene that's suffused with the kind of wit and intensity and vitriol that make actors want to play their parts with a fiery indignation worthy of an Academy Award.

So, now let's look at the rather tongue-in-cheek example of screenplay format that follows to see why and how screenwriters use those strange abbreviations and curious indentations to tell their story.

Sample Screenplay Format

```
INT. THE HAREM — DAY

Two dozen ODALISQUES lounge in the alabaster hall,
an undulating sea of pearl and ebony skins arrayed
on a brocaded empire of ottomans to await the
whims of pleasure.

Discreetly to one side, the intimidating bulk of
the HEAD EUNUCH surveys his charges with an impas-
sive scowl.  If not so much a man, he is never-
theless an enduring force as sinister as the
twisted yataghan that dangles from his oiled
nakedness.

THE CHIEF CONCUBINE

A woman with the dried-persimmon expression of
eternal scheming etched into her wizened face,
FATIMA THE BARREN suddenly pricks up her ears,
sensing the footsteps of her master.

THE HAREM

A rustle of airy silks and flickering eyelashes
focus on the bronzed doors as the Head Eunuch swings
open the barred portal for the entrance of —
```

THE CALIPH

ABDUL HAFEEZ ACHMET BEN VEREEN sweeps into the
room, flanked by his retinue of personal body-
guards.

Fatima trots over to pant hopefully at the feet
of her husband.

                    FATIMA
          What is your pleasure, my lord?

But the Caliph dismisses her with a wave of his
hand.

                    CALIPH
          At rest, little flowers. I visit my
          garden only to inhale the scent of
          your blossoms.
               (wryly)
          Your fruits are best plucked in the
          evening.

Flattering giggles echo through the room.

                    CALIPH
          Yet, like any prudent gardener, I
          wish to introduce a tender new
          growth to our orchard, that she may
          be nurtured in your care.

The Caliph beckons toward the corridor outside,
where a tinkle of ANKLE BELLS announces the
entrance of —

KHALIA

A dark, smoldering beauty insinuates itself into the harem.

                    CALIPH (V.O.)
          An exquisite rose from the south.

THE HAREM

An instant crackle of suspicion sparks through the Odalisques —

                    FATIMA
               (eyeing the rival)
          Be wary, my lord. Every rose has a
          thorn for a friend.

                                        CUT TO:

EXT. THE THIEVES' ENCAMPMENT — DAY

ALI SAID IBN BAD vaults into the silver-gilt saddle of his white stallion.

Elements of the Screenplay Format

```
INT. THE HAREM — DAY
```

Commonly called the *slug line* and set with the left margin about 1.5 inches from the left edge of the page, this portion of the scene description which contains the abbreviations "EXT." or "INT." for Exterior or Interior should be in all uppercase. It is a brief identification of the location in which the scene takes place. The slug line normally includes an indication of whether the scene takes place in DAY or NIGHT.

```
Two dozen ODALISQUES lounge in the alabaster hall,
an undulating sea of pearl and ebony skins arrayed
on a brocaded empire of ottomans to await the
whims of pleasure.
```

The *action description* immediately below the slug line is written in upper-and lowercase. It sets the action of the scene in more detail, often as a wide shot that establishes the setting as a whole. This action description is also used to introduce new characters, ODALISQUES, whose names appear in ALL CAPS the first time we see them. Thereafter, when the characters' names are used in scene description they appear in upper-and lowercase.

```
Discreetly to one side, the intimidating bulk of
the HEAD EUNUCH surveys his charges with an impas-
sive scowl. If not so much a man, he is never-
theless an enduring force as sinister as the
twisted yataghan that dangles from his oiled
nakedness.
```

If you have a particularly long action description, or you have more than one action to describe, you can skip a space between the elements to indicate to the reader that something else is going on. In the example above, a second new character, the HEAD EUNUCH, is introduced. He might be introduced in a separate shot, or he might walk through the shot of the harem, or the camera may hold on him for a moment while panning the entire harem. It is not important to indicate on the page exactly how the character is visually introduced. That is the director's job. It is only important to present the character to the reader in such a way that the reader recognizes the character and will remember that character later.

```
THE CHIEF CONCUBINE
A woman with the dried-persimmon expression of
eternal scheming etched into her wizened face,
FATIMA THE BARREN suddenly pricks up her ears,
sensing the footsteps of her master.
```

When a character is particularly important, you might want to introduce the character as a shot, that is, as an implied close-up. Again, how the director chooses to introduce the character is the director's decision, but as a screenwriter you are trying to influence the *reader*. Generally, contemporary selling scripts avoid using camera directions such as MS (medium shot) and CU (close-up), or angles such as CAMERA PANS RIGHT, or scene numbers. These are production elements that are added to the script at a much later date in the filmmaking process. Rather, you are writing a script which is designed to give the reader a conception of the story on paper, not an exact delineation of the photographic pictures on the screen.

In this case, the Chief Concubine is introduced both by her rank in the harem and by her name, FATIMA THE BARREN. More important, however, her character is given a metaphorical description and a characteristic action rather than a purely physical description. She might be thin or fat or short or tall. It makes no difference as long as she portrays the quality of "eternal scheming."

114

THE HAREM

A rustle of airy silks and flickering eyelashes
focus on the bronzed doors as the Head Eunuch swings
open the barred portal for the entrance of —

Here there is an *implied* return to the wide shot that opened the scene.
How the director chooses to make the transition is a determination
that will be made on the set and in the editing room, but for the sake
of the script, the screenwriter indicates to the reader that the scene is
moving on to a new element, especially by the use of the dash at the
end of the action description that leads the reader's eye directly to —

THE CALIPH

ABDUL HAFEEZ ACHMET BEN VEREEN sweeps into the
room, flanked by his retinue of personal body-
guards.

Again, by using a character as an implicit camera angle, the screenwriter calls the reader's attention to the new element, then immediately names the character and describes the action of what is clearly an
important person in this drama.

Fatima trots over to pant hopefully at the feet
of her husband.

Fatima now carries the action into the same "shot" as she sidles up to
her husband and speaks the first lines of dialogue in the scene.

                FATIMA
    What is your pleasure, my lord?

When the character's name is used as a dialogue heading it always appears in uppercase and centered on the page. The dialogue speech itself is set about one and a half inches in from left script margin, and about two inches in from right margin.

```
But the Caliph dismisses her with a wave of his
hand.
                     CALIPH
        At rest, little flowers.  I visit my garden
        only to inhale the scent of your blossoms.
```

It certainly isn't essential that the Caliph have an action of any kind at this point, and any good actor will determine whether a wave of the hand or a contemptuous look or nothing at all will best suit the character. The point, however, is to carry the force of the scene for the reader, not to give a literal blow-by-blow description of the physical gestures for the actor and director.

```
             (wryly)
        Your fruits are best plucked in the
        evening.
```

Many beginning screenwriters want to include a parenthetical line-reading direction (sometimes called a *wryly* because that's often what the cue indicates) on virtually every dialogue speech to instruct an actor on how to say a line. Needless to say, actors and directors find these authorial intrusions presumptuous and greatly resent them. The fact is, your intentions should be clear from the way the scene is written without any propping up from parenthetical directions. Only if the line is possibly ambiguous, as might be the case if a character were speaking to only one member of a larger group of people on screen, should you use a parenthetical linereading direction.

```
Flattering giggles echo through the room.

                    CALIPH

        Yet, like any prudent gardener, I
        wish to introduce a tender new growth
        to our orchard, that she may be
        nurtured in your care.
```

It is usually a good idea to separate your character's dialogue speeches into shorter chunks by breaking the dialogue with actions, especially when there is a particularly long speech that cannot fit on a single page. Shorter speeches help you control the rhythm of a page and, moreover, let the reader easily digest the speeches. When you do break up a character's speeches into several chunks, be sure to repeat the character's dialogue heading so that the reader knows who is talking, but it is entirely unnecessary to write "(More)" or "(Continued)" beside a character name. "(More)" and "(Continued)" are indications that are sometimes used in shooting scripts to avoid confusion in multiple production drafts where there are daily and even hourly changes. In your selling script these extraneous terms simply become obtrusive appurtenances on the page.

```
The Caliph beckons toward the corridor outside,
where a tinkle of ANKLE BELLS announces the
entrance of —
```

Specific sound cues such as ANKLE BELLS are written in uppercase only if they are important to the scene as indications of something significant about to arrive on screen. Ordinary ambient noises are not usually considered sound cues since they are merely texture and do not signify any particular change in attention. If a character were sitting alone in his room, for instance, the sound of traffic noise outside would be unimportant. However, if that character is anticipating the hit men who are coming to murder him, the sound cue CAR DOOR SLAMS out front could be vital as a signal of change to come.

                              KHALIA
A dark, smoldering beauty insinuates itself into
the harem.

                          CALIPH (V.O.)
          An exquisite rose from the south.

Again the screenwriter uses an implied shot to introduce a character
on the page, but this time there is an added element. The Caliph
introduces the character (**V.O.**), meaning **Voice Over**. Voice Over
indicates that a character who is not seen on screen is speaking in dialogue, or narration, or thought, or a tape recording, or on a telephone
or radio, is speaking *over* the image that the audience sees. A similar
technique is (**O.S.**), meaning **Off Screen**, which is used to indicate the
sound of something of importance or a character voice that is about to
arrive on screen or that is occurring off screen to draw the character's
attention. An explosion may occur, for instance, off screen, which
causes the characters to leap up from their breakfast at the diner and
run outside to see what's happened. These indications of sound and
dialogue directional focus should be used in your script with great
restraint. They are techniques that may help you tell a story to a reader,
but they can also confuse a reader if not used skillfully, and ordinarily the
decision of whether or not to use (V.O.) or (O.S.) to enhance a scene is
made in the editing stage long after the shooting of the film is finished.

THE HAREM

An instant crackle of suspicion sparks through the
Odalisques —

                            FATIMA
                     (eyeing the rival)
          Be wary, my lord. Every rose has
          a thorn for a friend.

                              118

Now we've reached a fine line of definition. Is "**(eyeing the rival)**" a substantive comment to help the writer tell the story to the reader, or is it an uncalled-for direction to the actress? In this case, it contributes to the overall sense of enviousness and distrust in the harem, and helps set the tension that carries over into the next master scene. As a writer, you need to constantly ask yourself whether you really need all the filigree you have on the page to help you tell the story and set the context — or are some things merely self-indulgent arabesques.

                                                              CUT TO:

It is rarely necessary to indicate anything except "CUT TO:," "DISSOLVE TO:," or "FADE TO:" between master scenes. Generally, "CUT TO:" indicates a simple change of time and location; "DISSOLVE TO:" indicates a greater time change or a greater change of mood; and "FADE TO:" is used to indicate an extreme change of time such as many years. The actual film may use a different device to indicate time and mood shift, but the significant function of these devices on the written page is to help the reader notice that the story is moving from one master scene to another. For this reason, it is a good idea to leave *lots of white space* surrounding your transition. Skip at least three spaces before and after the transitional element before you begin the new scene to be absolutely certain the reader's eye recognizes the transition. Nothing is worse for a reader than to suddenly discover they are in a new master scene and have no idea when or how they got there.

EXT. THE THIEVES' ENCAMPMENT — DAY

ALI SAID IBN BAD vaults into the silver-gilt saddle of his white stallion.

Now the script moves into a new master scene. This one takes place outside in the daylight in a wholly new location with a completely new set of characters. With any luck, Fatima's preceding line, "Be wary,

119

my lord. Every rose has a thorn for a friend," introduces a tension into this scene so that the audience anticipates that something dramatic is going to happen. And, after all, that's the screenwriter's job — to make something happen.

Scribble Exercise:

❏ In addition to the main character and the antagonist, are there one or two other characters who are absolutely essential to tell your screen story?

❏ Briefly describe ten to twelve master scenes in which the main character, the antagonist, or another essential character appear, and which you *must have* to tell your story. These are the broad scenes which have continuity of thought and action that advance the story by setting a problem or resolving a conflict; they are the episodes that form the cause-and-effect backbone of your story.

THE AESTHETIC — GUIDING THE READER'S HEART

Now that there is a structurally sound building fabricated from necessary materials, held together by indispensable rivets and mortar, and existing in an encompassing milieu, let's concentrate on the aesthetic form or *style* the building takes.

Style in screenwriting is the tonal expression of the context. It is the way the writer indicates to the reader *how* to read the screenplay. One of the most common complaints among Hollywood screenwriters is that their screenplays were misread, that their hilarious comedies were read as tragedies, or their fervent social commentaries were taken as satires. Well, for the most part, the fault lies with the writer. The writer has to tell the reader how to read the screenplay.

Scribble Exercise:

❏ What is the very first scene description in your script?

❏ How does this scene description give a clue to the reader about the way the screenplay should be read? What do you tell the reader about the context of your story in this first scene?

SCENE DESCRIPTIONS — LESS IS MORE

Scenes tell stories. Like small-scale dramas, each scene in a film has a beginning, middle, and end. And, like the larger drama that the scene contributes to, you want to bring the reader into the scene at the point of greatest interest, but you want to get out of the scene before the conflict has been completely resolved. This ongoing sense of being not-quite-finished contributes tension and energy to the drama, driving it forward toward the real dramatic conclusion.

```
INT. THE CABIN — NIGHT

Marti rolls out of bed.  She cracks open the win-
dow to let in the delta night.

                    MARTI
          Stinks out there.

                    SENATOR GEORGE
          Then close the damn window.

                    MARTI
          Smells like something died.

                    SENATOR GEORGE
          Honeybunch, y'all just c'mon back
          to bed and you won't have to worry
          about nothing being dead, I promise
          you.

                    MARTI
          I want to go see.  I want to see
          what died.
```

She climbs through the window and picks her way
over the moonlit landscape of crackling driftwood.

                    SENATOR GEORGE
          Little girl, c'mon back. I paid
          for 'round-the-world, you know.

Marti reaches the line of cypress trees. Sen.
George hauls himself out of bed and swaddles the
damp sheet around his middle.

                    SENATOR GEORGE
          Aw, shucks.

SEN. GEORGE CLIMBS AWKWARDLY THROUGH WINDOW

picks his way barefoot over the gnarled carpet of
razor-edged fronds.

                    SENATOR GEORGE
          Goddammit. What a man's gotta go
          through for a little poontang once
          and a while.

Marti stands in a clearing beneath the cypress.
She stares intently at something on the ground.

                    MARTI
          I found what's dead.

                    SENATOR GEORGE
          Good. Let's throw it in the water
          and get back to the house.

She hunkers and reaches out to touch the shape-
less mound of fur at her feet. It moves. Marti
jerks back.

                    MARTI
        It's not dead!

She bends to pick up the little thing.

                    MARTI
        Lookit. It's a baby animal.

The toga-clad senator waddles up to dispense justice.

                SENATOR GEORGE
        Shoot, it's just a raccoon. Better
        put it back before the mother comes
        along looking for it.

Marti cradles the baby fur to her bare breasts.

                    MARTI
        No. No. This baby's mommy ran off
        an' left it. She's not coming back.

                SENATOR GEORGE
        Huh?

                    MARTI
        I can tell. If I leave it alone, it'll
        die. It'll just curl up here and die.

                SENATOR GEORGE
        Well what do you expect me to do?
        Take it back to bed with us?

```
                    MARTI
     No.   Take me home.   I'm going to
     keep this baby alive myself.   I'll be
     the mommy.

                 SENATOR GEORGE
     Now look here, little girl.   I paid my
     money and I want my satisfaction.

                    MARTI
     You… you can keep the money.   All
     of it.   Just take me and him back to
     town.   That's all I want.

                 SENATOR GEORGE
     Aw shucks.   I come all the way out
     here for some beaver and all I get's
     a little 'coon.

                                    CUT TO:
```

Each scene in your screenplay should do two things simultaneously:

1. **Drive the plot forward by giving the reader *new* information.** Every scene must provide the audience with something they do not already know about the story. This is not to say that you cannot clarify ambiguous points, such as in a mystery, but the clarification must also serve to further the evolution of the puzzle.

2. **Reveal something more about the main character.** Characters who stay fixed are uninteresting. Remember that the drama is about the change your main character makes by coming to grips with the internal need. That change arrives incrementally, so the audience needs to continually learn a little bit more about the character with each decision the character takes.

127

In contrast, the weakest kind of scene is one in which nothing at all happens. All too often, beginning screenwriters become enamored of the scenes they see in their heads, usually a detailed pictorial likeness of some experience they've lived that they mistakenly believe contributes authenticity to a drama.

```
INT. HOTEL ROOM — DAY
```

Martha sits on the edge of the bed in a small hotel room with very high ceilings. The room contains a double bed with a Laura Ashley spread, two overstuffed chairs, a large antique dresser and a brand new television with remote control. The hallway has a mirrored closet with sliding doors. Along the back is the bathroom.

The SOUND OF SHAVING comes from the bathroom accompanied by George's occasional humming.

> MARTHA
> This is nice, don't you think?

No answer.

> MARTHA
> George.

George's head pops out of the wall in front of the bathroom. He has shaving cream on his face.

> GEORGE
> Did you say something, Martha?

He ducks his head back in. The SOUND OF THE WATER stops.

>   MARTHA
>   I was saying this hotel is nice.
>   Don't you think?

George pops his head out again. The shaving cream
is gone. He is clean shaven.

>   GEORGE
>   Yes, it is nice.

George pops his head back in the bathroom and
starts the SOUND OF SHAVING again. Martha sits
on the edge of the bed. She leans over and plays
with the television, attempting to find something
to watch.

Absolutely nothing happens in this scene. We learn nothing about the
characters and the plot does not move forward. Furthermore, we have
thoroughly unnecessary descriptions of furniture and completely irrelevant sound cues having to do with shaving. It is truly a scene without meaning for anyone except the screenwriter.

It is a common mistake for screenwriters to try to create on the page
what literally happens on screen. Remember that your craft is to evoke
imagery, not to describe pictures. You want to create an essence, a sen-
sation of action, not an exact delineation of what happens on screen.

THE SNOWMOBILE

plunges through vacant sky. A daredevil high-dive.
Drills toward the valley floor below, until —

SLAM!   It impacts solid ground with a jaw-shat-
tering wallop!

MARTHA

catapults off.   Face first into a snowbank.
Buried up to her ass.

GEORGE

still grips the throttles.   Rights the snowmobile.
Shoots off down the valley floor away, leaving —

MARTHA

who shakes herself loose from the snowbank. A
drenched spaniel.   Just in time to see —

THE SAAMI TROOPS

high-jump over the hidden ridge on skis and snow-
boards.

A dozen soldiers sail over Martha's head   Take
off after George. But as the next trooper hurtles
the ledge —

MARTHA

snatches the astonished man right off his snowboard.   Tosses him into the embankment.

Hardly a break in her stride.   Martha mounts the
captured snowboard.   Zips down the hillside.

COL. TRYGVE'S HELICOPTER

Col. Trygve sees his quarry escaping.

He lets loose another rocket. ZAP!

Blows away a snow bridge ahead of George.

The snowmobile snaps a new course.

Exactly how the director handles the action in this partial scene will depend on factors that the screenwriter cannot know at the time of the writing, so it is pointless to try to write the literal sequence of events. Instead, the screenwriter writes cause-and-effect action, a scene with a beginning, middle, and end that gives the reader a *rhythmic sense* of what will be on the screen. The screenwriter tries to create excitement on the page that suggests, but cannot duplicate, the excitement that can be recreated on the screen.

To be sure, not all scenes are exciting, at least visually. Inevitably there will be eating scenes, telephone conversations, and driving-in-the-car scenes which contain essential plot or character information but which are not in themselves visually dramatic. These are scenes for which the director and actors must take responsibility for the imagery. As a screenwriter, you provide the dramatic basis for the actors' facial expressions and gestures that are the particular visual genius of film. In these circumstances, don't even try to provide anything more on the page than the barest indication of the scene setting.

INT. GEORGE AND MARTHA'S HOUSE

George answers the telephone.
                    GEORGE
        Hello.

                    MARTHA (V.O.)
        You two-timing son-of-a-bitch!

131

INTERCUTTING GEORGE AND MARTHA

                    GEORGE
          Martha, where are you?

                    MARTHA
          Right where you left me, you jerk!

In this way, the screenwriter has not encroached on the discretion of the director and, more important, has made the scene easy to read by not cluttering it with superfluous visual cues.

Speaking of a jumble of visuals, some of the hardest scenes to write are the most obvious. Sex scenes, like fight scenes and car chase scenes, can easily become clichés. The temptation is to simply leave the scene up to the director and actors to improvise. However, the screenwriter needs to provide the actors and director with the contours for the scene in order to maintain the context that has been established throughout the script.

THE TURRET STAIRCASE

Slow, steady footsteps mount the staircase, spiral with the stone wall. Climb the iron ladder
through the open trap door of the turret.

IN THE LIGHTHOUSE TURRET

Preternatural eyes stare back from the shadows.
Martha's feral form crouches at the base of the
lighthousing.

```
George explodes from the open hatchway.   Martha
uncoils,  rises  eagerly  to  match  his  oncoming
embrace.   Throws herself into him.

Her talons claw into his flesh.

His thrusts drive her back against the inner rail-
ing.   The warmth of her body instantly fogs an
imprint on the glass.  Repeatedly sucks and slides
against the thick, frosted panes. Strobe together
with the lightning flashes.  Her low moan escapes
into the storm.  Mingles with the howl of the wind
stroking the cleft turret facets as —

OUTSIDE

— splintered images of the two steaming bodies
refract out to sea from the aged lighthouse.

                              DISSOLVE TO:
```

Of course, it is sometimes both possible and desirable, as we will see later, to take an otherwise strictly expository scene and make it perform several chores at once by placing it in a visually interesting setting.

The goal of every scene you write is to *make something happen*. You want to drive deeper into the characters and further into the plot. But if those were the only goals of screenwriting, then the indictment that screenwriting is only a blueprint would not be far from the truth. We could say, "This happens, and the character reacts that way, and then that happens and the character reacts this way." It might be a fairly accurate list of story elements, but it would certainly be a dull document to read, and it would be completely devoid of style. The screenwriter would have abdicated any responsibility for contributing context and cohesive story to the ultimate picture.

133

In some respects, this abandonment has been taking place in Hollywood for some time because of the ascendancy of the director as the *author* of a film. But, except for those very special filmmakers like Woody Allen or Joel and Ethan Coen who are truly responsible for the total creation of their films, movies always begin with a screenwriter — someone who faces a blank page and creates something out of nothing.

Scribble Exercise:

❏ Write a two-page chase scene, fight scene, or sex scene *without dialogue* that contains a clear beginning, middle, and end.

❏ Write a two-page scene *without dialogue* of a married couple entering their house or apartment immediately after it has been burglarized.

DIALOGUE — "SPIRITS FROM THE VASTY DEEP"

One of the most frequent questions asked by beginning screenwriters is "How do I write good dialogue?" The answer is — learn how to listen. The great Irish playwright J.M. Synge, author of *The Playboy of the Western World* and *Riders to the Sea*, spent years listening to the dialects of the peasants of Ireland, including eavesdropping through a chink in the floor of a country house to the unique speech of the kitchen servant girls. He trained his ear to the rhythms of the characters he wanted to write about. While you may not have to spend years in prison or on a ship or in space just to get the dialogue rhythms down, you should make a conscious effort to *hear* how people speak, the phrasing, vocabulary, and rhythmic structure they use to express themselves.

Dialogue has two functions: to move the story forward, and to reveal character. It is often said that film is a visual medium, but characters are vocal creatures and writing is about words, not pictures. Certain kinds of pure or experimental cinema, or film used as a medium for recording dance or some other art form, may exist without dialogue, but ever since 1927's *The Jazz Singer*, feature films have been *talkies*. In everyday life, talking is our major means of communication. It is little wonder, then, that we naturally expect the characters in film to use the same communication skills we do. The difference is, characters use that skill of talking so much better than we do. Think of all the famous lines throughout movie history, from Mae West's "Why don't you come up and see me sometime?" to Arnold Swarzenegger's "Hasta la vista, Baby." A screenwriter gave that character exactly the right line to say at exactly the right time. Instead, in life we often seem to fumble for the right thing to say, squirming in our own inarticulateness, apprehension, embarrassment, or hostility.

Subtext

And, oddly enough, it is that same wordless anxiety that underlies the best dialogue. Yes, the best dialogue consists of the things the characters don't say — William Shakespeare's "spirits from the vasty deep," the uneasy monsters that glide just beneath the surface of what is said. In virtually every scene, even those delivering the most prosaic expository information, there is something the characters aren't telling each other, something they are afraid of. It is this underlying fear that contributes dramatic tension to the scene and provides for character revelation as well as plot development. Characters may be more eloquent than we are in real life, but they are no less apprehensive, especially when it comes to emotional risk.

The opposite of subtext is dialogue that is overly obvious, usually called *on-the-nose* dialogue, and that expresses information the characters or the audience already knows. It's this kind of dialogue that gives us lines like "As I've already told you..." and "Look, he has a gun!" which are, at best, poor writing or, more charitably, attempts to smooth over poor directing. There are a couple of exceptions to the on-the-nose dialogue prohibition, though, two lines that will occur in nearly every movie no matter what the subject matter or genre: "What do you want?" and "Are you all right?" The line "What do you want?" is probably necessary in even the best-written screenplays to give the main character or antagonist a chance to clearly state the goal to the reader. In the actual film, the line may be replaced by some action, but it is often necessary in the script to make sure the reader knows why the characters are doing what they are doing. Likewise, the line "Are you all right?" is virtually inevitable in any film. Drama is conflict. Conflict has consequences. Consequences are often damaging. So, whether the character has fallen out of an airplane or out of love, some other character will, in due time, ask, "Are you all right?"

*E*nergy

Every scene provides the audience with new information. For the most part, that information comes through dialogue. But information itself, especially the kind of expository information that is often necessary to set up a story or to move it forward, is not inherently energetic. In fact, the most efficient way to deliver such information might be to hand the audience members written program notes as is often done in theatrical productions. However, although movies may not be about efficiency, they are about getting on with the story in an active, energetic manner. This means that the dialogue is *lean*, to the point. Unlike life, movie dialogue drives toward a conclusion, avoids chitchat, and for the most part stays away from long, preachy, moralizing speeches. There are some filmmakers whose work is characterized by nothing so much as preachy moralizing speeches, but they are the exception. Most of the audience wants to get on with the story, and that means getting into the scene after it starts and getting out before it's finished, leapfrogging the energy from one scene to the next.

But how do you infuse energy into purely expository dialogue? By placing it in an unexpected setting. Carry on the exposition during a bowling match, a car chase, or a bedroom scene. Film has a particular genius for being able to deliver information and emotion to the audience at several different levels simultaneously with music, sound effects, picture, and dialogue. Imagine George and Martha making plans for their upcoming wedding reception and arguing about which family members can or cannot be seated next to each other — while the two of them break into a jewelry store to steal their diamond ring sets. Now add that they're unaware that they've triggered the silent alarm. And the cop who's responding to the call is Martha's brother-in-law. The one who owes George $10,000. The ordinary expository dialogue that might have been conducted at the kitchen table becomes part of a much more significant scene with many more possibilities for dramatic complication.

138

𝒳pectation

It's the sense of risk that imparts expectation to the dialogue scene. Ask yourself what the characters are in conflict about. Remember self-concept? What does each character have to risk in the scene? What is at stake for each individual? What could each individual lose or gain?

So, as you have no doubt figured out by now, the secret to good dialogue, Subtext, Energy, and eXpectation — is **SEX**. That is the best mnemonic you can work with for writing good dialogue. The tension, anticipation, energy, excitement, apprehension, fun, risk, and satisfaction of sex is analogous to the best of movie dialogue.

Of course, some of the worst dialogue can follow the same pattern.


```
Afterward, Jorge experiences an inner exaltation
coupled with pride and contentment.

                    JORGE
        I was the first.  The first man in
        your life, wasn't I?

                    MARTA
        Yes.

                    JORGE
        Why didn't you tell me?

                    MARTA
        Why?  Was it important?
```

139

                    JORGE
    Of course, now I will have to marry
    you.

                    MARTA
    (feeling her cheeks grow hot)
        Don't tease. I did not take our
        lovemaking lightly.

                    JORGE
    Nor I.

His arms go about her and he pulls her close.

                    MARTA
    (bursting with happiness)
        How old are you, Jorge?

                    JORGE
    Twenty-three.

                    MARTA
    Tell me about yourself.

                    JORGE
    The usual story. Father dead,
    mother left with a shack full of
    children. Being the eldest, I had
    to support them.

                    MARTA
    Is that why you became a matador?

                    JORGE
    Who can say? Why did you decide to be
    a ballerina?

                    140

Scribble Exercise:

❏ CONTENT: Write a two-page male/female dialogue scene. It can be set with characters of any age in any era, at any time and place, but it must begin with the line "What do you want?" and end with the line "Are you all right?"

❏ SUBTEXT: Rewrite the same scene, but in this version, except for the first and last lines, you may not use any pronouns (*I, you, we, they, them, it, this, that, those, etc.*, as in *"We've already done it."* or *"These are what they need."* or *"Give me that."*).

❏ RISK: Continue to rewrite the same scene, but now you must eliminate all negative statements involving *don't, can't, won't, shouldn't*, etc.

❏ ENERGY: Tape record ten minutes of conversation between two people. Transcribe the conversation verbatim. You will have approximately ten pages of *realspeak*. Edit these ten pages down to two pages of dialogue.

❏ RHYTHM: Transcribe a section of dialogue from a screenplay you admire. Copy two pages *by hand* (not on a typewriter or computer) to get a kinesthetic feel for the rhythm in which the characters speak.

❏ RHYTHM: Write a two-page, two-character dialogue scene using *only the following vocabulary words*:

ahulii
amoroso
ancheta
anjozian
aquilino
argaman
argentieri
arriola
arzaga
asch
bajinting
barreca
batkouic
baur
beharry
beletsky
benzvi
bercsi
berkel
biczo
bivens
bonfa
bork
bova
brasch
brotslaw
burawski
caddwallader
calvi
campo
caothien
cauble
chaix
chambers
chau

chichocki
cho
clymer
coco
coe
cohodes
cunliffe
dalrymple
daunais
ditmars
dvorak
dymalski
fibish
finnsdottir
foss
fragale
fund
gindi
gion
gorn
guenon
hawes
heebner
higiinglove
huey
jablow
jahromi
kahane
karabees
kohatsu
kohn
kreng
kriel
kross
kusnadi

lame
locurcio
lopin
mann
michalek
neunecker
oura
pai
platz
reis
salvo
schenz
schnall
schorr
sintay
stiffler
stumpe
syrmis
tait
tan
teeling
thum
todoroff
tognozzi
torgove
truitt
tuch
umber
uram
uytana
veevaert
wendt
wojnar
yevenes
yu

zicree
zorn
zrinyi

Chapter Eight

GETTING DOWN TO IT — WRITING YOUR SCREENPLAY

"Creation is a great wheel. It does not move without crushing something."

— Victor Hugo

The issue of talent in writing is greatly overrated. Some people have what seems to be an innate ability to tell stories; some are great at making up jokes; some seem to have a knack for character.

Good writing is about instinct — but it is an instinct that you *earn* by doing. Good writing is about putting words together over and over and over again until you're absolutely satisfied that they convey to a reader what your soul intends to say.

Most of us begin by seeing a distant mirage. Perhaps it is a mirage of a character, or a place, or a scene, or a theme we want to explore. This fugitive hallucination bobbles and cavorts in our heads until we begin to get some kind of fix on it, an attachment that suddenly transforms the reverie into the zero-gravity elation of a *Precious Vision*. Instantly, we can see the whole story at once. Everything falls into place so neatly! It's brilliant. The perfect screenplay!

Unfortunately for many writers, the Precious Vision is the beginning and end of their writing life. They never take the vision from their heads to the paper because to do so would be to shatter the illusion and actually have to make the vision work. As long as the illusion remains clamped in your head, of course, it is never pressured to reach an audience. But as soon as you set out to communicate that idea to others, you must make some hard decisions — and the great clanking wheel of creativity will begin its inexorable crush.

> **We Get Mail!**
> I have an unbelievable screenplay that is fresh and original. No one can even come close to the screenplay that I have started. The only problem is that it is so difficult to write the complicated scenes.

Getting past the Precious Vision usually means settling into some serious *Couch Writing*. Now, this is a tough phase, because your family and friends are going to accuse you of wasting time and lollygagging around with a dazed look in your eye and the sporadic unintelligible mumble that escapes from your lips. You will be condemned for the good-for-nothing loafer everyone always knew you were. Nothing, of course, could be farther from the truth. You are, in fact, writing. You are musing, envisioning, and resonating your way toward the premise statement of your screenplay — what's it all about. Just what is the *story* you're going to tell?

However, if you've used your Couch Writing time productively, you are probably ready to put your fingers on the keys or grasp a pencil and start creating the all-important *Screenplay Outline*. This is the "Astrolabe draft." Like the ancient clockwork mechanism for marking celestial bodies, the Screenplay Outline is a device that will guide you on your journey from the beginning through the middle to the end of the uncharted screenplay universe. The constellations in that universe are immense connect-the-dots images. The brightest stars are easily seen, and from them you must be able to interpolate the connecting bodies that create icons out of the astral soup.

Each writer creates a Screenplay Outline in their own fashion, and you will have to experiment until you find the technique that suits your personal habits. Some writers like to use note cards, jotting down scenes and bits of dialogue which they can then rearrange continually until they are satisfied with the structure. Other writers use chalk or white boards to diagram overall act structures like oscillograms. Many writers work with partners so that they can talk and argue out the points of a story, testing and refining the cause-and-effect reasoning for each character action before they set the work on paper. Many writers have to sit down and do a kind of preliminary draft of the story. Sometimes this preliminary outline draft is in screenplay form, sometimes in paragraph-prose form like a short story, and sometimes a hybrid of the two that may run for two or three hundred pages. This type of outline process, however, is merely a way for the writer to begin to talk to the page, and should never be mistaken for the creation of the screenplay itself.

" *The hard part is getting to the top of page 1.*"

— Tom Stoppard

During the Couch Writing phase, you've made notes of impressions, scenes, dialogue, characters, etc. You've already begun to organize in your mind the overall shape the screenplay needs to have. You know the main character, the antagonist, what they're fighting about, and what the ending of the story is. Whether the initial outline takes the form of note cards, a sheet of paper, a tape recording, or a chalk board schematic, its job is to configure those elements into a convincing story. During the actual writing of the screenplay, the mechanics of how a scene works or even the order of the scenes themselves may change, but the overall infrastructure of the piece is laid down in this outline — and without a solid outline you will never find your way through the astral miasma.

```
┌─────────────────────────────────────────────┐
│                                               │
│  We Get Mail!                                 │
│  I started to write this adventure movie      │
│  script but I'm having some difficulties on   │
│  how to write down my ideas.                  │
│                                               │
└─────────────────────────────────────────────┘
```

Now you can begin writing. With a solid outline in place, you are now ready to do a *Story Draft* of the screenplay. There are two possible versions of this Story Draft, and it's quite possible that you will want to do both.

Most writers do a *Prose Treatment* of their screenplay at some point. A Prose Treatment is written in the form of a short story except that it is always in present tense like a screenplay. The treatment may be only a few pages or very detailed depending on whether it is a device for the writer's own use or a selling device offered to interest a producer in reading the complete screenplay.

More commonly at this stage, you will begin to write a *First Draft Screenplay*, the parenthetical dialogue draft where the writer includes absolutely *everything* in literal detail from the imagination. Don't hold back, just get it down on paper. If you feel compelled to list the pieces of furniture in the room, do it. If you must assign a "wryly" to every character speech, do it. If you have to describe the costumes the characters wear down to the last Ralph Lauren handkerchief and nose ring, do it. Whatever it takes to get the story out of your head and onto the page, away from the Precious Vision and into the practical realm of screen storytelling, get to work and do it.

"What is written without effort is in general read without pleasure."
— Samuel Johnson

During this draft, if you haven't already, you will probably find yourself researching context elements of time, place, and artifact. You may also have to pause in the writing of the First Draft in order to write a Character Study or a Context Study because you find that you're stumped about where the story goes or a character you thought you knew simply refuses to cooperate. That's okay. Stop. Put the First Draft aside and write a Character Study to free up that character. Do whatever you have to do to explore and research your subject matter, your story, your characters, and your context. This First Draft is the time to answer all those questions that were vast dark spaces between the bright stars on the outline.

How many pages have you turned out for the First Draft? Hundreds. At least. In fact, the designation *First Draft* is misleading. It implies that there is only one First Draft when, in fact, there may be several. You continue to rewrite the First Draft until you've ironed out all of the problems, all of the audience's unasked questions, all of the unclear character motivations, and all of the scene transitions that carry the reader easily through the story.

```
We Get Mail!
I'd just like to say it's very frustrating as
an   unrecognized   screenwriter,   (very   good
screenwriter, I might add) who has to see some
of the complete trash put out by studios today.
All my work is so much better than that and if
they'd just invest money into discovering all
the potential talent that must be out there
instead of plundering yet another dire roman-
tic/action comedy from the system, I'm sure
the world would be a better place.
```

Now you can begin writing. This is the *Editing Draft*. First, you eliminate all of the parenthetical dialogue cues, the "wrylies" that tell actors how to read the line. Next, you eliminate all of the unnecessary descriptions in scenes. Ruthlessly ask yourself if we really need to know how many chairs are in the room or what brand of underwear the main character wears? Have no mercy with yourself. Cut. Slash. Rewrite. Less is more. Fewer words. Less description. More expressive imagery.

Go on an *ING* hunt. Set your word processor to find the ubiquitous *ing* verb ending. Instead of "George is looking out the window," write "George looks out the window." Instead of "George was seen by the police," write "The police see George." Film is *now*, direct. Screenplays must also be immediate.

"A writer is someone for whom writing is more difficult than it is for other people."

— Thomas Mann

While you're playing with your word processor, check, double-check, and triple-check your spelling and grammar. Visually proofread a hard copy of your script for grammatical and spelling errors that the computer can't discern. Your high school English teacher was right, correct grammar and spelling do matter! If you want to write professionally, the script must look professional!

```
We Get Mail!
I'm the best writer that you will ever come
across and I wan't (sic) to get started RIGHT
NOW! I wan't to write, I wan't to see it up
on the big screen and I wan't to make money!
```

148

Now you can begin writing. Let's call this the *Agent's Draft*, that is, the version of the script that you're finally prepared to have other people read. Until this draft, you should not have shown any of your work on this script to anyone else. You are *not* ready to put the script into the marketplace yet, but you can judiciously select several people to read your script for feedback. These readers should be good critics, knowledgeable about screenwriting and articulate in their critiques. They should be able to focus on particular points that will make your work better rather than offering generalizations such as, "You've got really great characters except for that one guy in the beginning." You need very specific notes that will help you rewrite the screenplay for clarity of plot and depth of character. You do not want to offer this draft of the screenplay to your mother, your best friend, your business partner, or your spouse unless they are practiced critics with experience in screenplay writing.

> **We Get Mail!**
> If you just wrote a blockbuster, and you had never written anything before, who would get the first copy and how long would you wait for them to buy it?

Now you can begin writing. Incorporate everything you've learned from your critic-colleagues to rewrite your screenplay into a *Market Draft*. This is the selling screenplay we've been talking about, the document that the reader picks up and cannot put down, the compelling story that demands to be made into a motion picture, the bundle of pages that is going to launch your career as a professional screenwriter.

But first, before we talk about the actual marketing of that screenplay, let's take a brief look at what it means to be a screenwriter.

We Get Mail!

I am a new screenwriter who has just finished his first screenplay. I am very fond
of it, everyone who has read it is very fond
of it. My problem is that it is a very artistic, dark screenplay that is put together
very differently, something that only a
director who wanted to make something new
and original could understand doing. I have
a strong feeling that this won't make it
very far with agents due to the darkness and
originality of it, they won't want to take
a chance. What should I do?

THE WRITER'S LIFE

Writing is the most frightening profession you can undertake. Oh,
sure, rescuing a kitten from a burning building, or topping off a skyscraper, or plunking down a few mil on the latest IPO may cause you
to catch your breath once or twice, but writing is really terrifying.
At least with the kitten, the skyscraper, and the IPO, you'll know you
have an obvious, unmistakable success or failure. Writing is always
uncertain. Even at its best, it never quite matches that Precious Vision
that began the process. The product is always in some respect a compromise. Perhaps the compromise that results from the creative decisions you've had to make along the way produces a far superior work
than that capricious hallucination of your fantasy, but the written page
is never quite the same unflawed daydream child it was before craft
brought it into the world.

"I always do the first line well, but I have trouble doing the others."
— Molière

150

Every time you face the blank page, then, the potential for failure is enormously high, perhaps even inevitable. We're not talking about popular or economic nonsuccess here, but real personal deficiency, the kind of naked truth that jerks you awake in a cold sweat at night. We're talking about *I'm-a-fraud-and-everybody-knows-it* failure. That is what makes writing the most terrifying profession.

This is the reason why many would-be writers never get around to putting anything down on paper. It is also the reason why so many people who wouldn't presume to fly their own airliner or perform their own hemorrhoid surgery or even mow their own grass are absolutely certain they can do a better job of writing than a professional writer — *after* that writer has knocked back the blank page to create a work of something from a beginning of nothing.

Being a writer of any sort is linked to poor mental health, according to a British psychiatrist. Dr. Felix Post studied biographies of 100 writers and reported that poets had more mood swings and manic depression requiring hospitalization than authors or playwrights, but they were less likely to die young or be promiscuous. Only 31% of the poets were alcoholics, compared to 54% of playwrights.

According to his study, psychosis or depression was evident in 80% of poets, 80.5% of novelists and 87.5% of playwrights. Half the poets failed to ever achieve "complete sexual union," while 42% of playwrights were known for their sexual promiscuity.

— British Journal of Psychiatry, as reported in the Los Angeles Times, May 2, 1996

So why would anyone willingly subject themselves to the distress and animosity of being a writer? That is exactly the question asked by George Orwell, the author of *1984* and *Animal Farm*.

Writers are all vain, selfish and lazy, and at the very bottom of their motives there lies a mystery. Writing is a horrible, exhausting experience, like a long bout of some painful illness. One would never undertake such a thing if one were not driven on by some demon whom one can neither resist nor understand.
— George Orwell, Why I Write, 1947

Orwell said, "Putting aside the need to earn a living ... there are four great motives for writing."

1. **Sheer Egoism** — The desire to seem clever, to be talked about, to be remembered after death, to get your own back on the grownups who snubbed you in childhood.

2. **Aesthetic Enthusiasm** — The perception of beauty in words and their right arrangement. Pleasure in the impact of one sound on another, ... in the rhythm of a good story.

3. **Historical Impulse** — The desire to see things as they are, to find out true facts and store them up for posterity ... to take pleasure in useless scraps of information.

4. **Political Purpose** — Using the word "political" in the widest possible sense, the desire to push the world in a certain direction.

Sound familiar? Of course.

Like other artists, writers would be less than honest if we didn't admit that our own self-concept is very much bound up in the act of creation. Even though most of us write because we are compelled to do so by Orwell's "demon," we'd like to have the acclaim for what we do. But, of course, so would politicians, exotic dancers, and zoo keepers. For screenwriters this is a particularly tricky motivation, however. Most of us have discovered that we simply are not very good team players. We tend to be loners who aren't equipped to work for other people or on other people's time schedules. And yet, the predicament is that those are often the very same people to whom we need to demonstrate that we are worthy of their approval.

"Whenever you write, whatever you write, never make the mistake of assuming the audience is any less intelligent than you are."
— Rod Serling

The result is that screenwriters often define ourselves as apart from our audience and take on an *us-against-them* mentality. We make the audience less intelligent, less sensitive, less honorable than we are. This is the greatest mistake you can make as a screenwriter. That mass audience is composed of people who respond to the same emotional hooks you do, and if you want to be listened to, you have to speak to them. Good storytellers never separate themselves from their audience. A good storyteller is the enthralling voice from the firelight, not the bellow from the mountain high.

"If a writer has to rob his mother, he will not hesitate; the "Ode on a Grecian Urn" is worth any number of old ladies."
— William Faulkner

Writers love what they do. They play games with words and ideas. They finesse concepts on paper, and they take genuine pleasure in beguiling the reader. Of course, writing is not always fun, any more than practicing pushups or musical scales is fun, but it is always a challenge to be met, a game to be outwitted. Athletes frequently talk of being in love with their game whether or not they are star players. Writers are in love with their games as well, returning to the keyboard every day to pound out a new sentence, a new combination of words, a fresh inflection of meaning, or a brilliant evocation of mood that makes a screenplay sit up and whistle. We look for those moments of aesthetic matrimony where our vision and our craft suddenly come together. Fourth word in the side pocket. Whack! The rhythm of a good story. Rack 'em up again.

Even if we are not historians as such, all writers try to make sense out of the world they live in. We are naturally inclined to squeeze time and select events, to digest the chaos of the world and bring it to heel. It's Orwell's "historical impulse" that drives us to save snatches of information in our heads or scraps of paper or computer files, and then find ourselves completely delighted like children discovering forgotten toys in the attic when those tidbits appear on the page. But unlike true, academic historians, fiction writers must always be open to the surprises that make writing such an exhilarating experience. If you listen for the potential twists and nuances of a story or character, chances are the answer will be inside of you. Stories that we sometimes thought would be gloomy tragedies turn out to be sparkling farce. And there is nothing better than to get up in the morning and read yesterday's output with a fresh eye, as if, while you slept, the elves in your workshop hammered together a delightful surprise.

Naturally, all of us who write have an intention, like Orwell, to proclaim our political or social wisdom. Often in our passion we expect to use the power of cinema to change the world overnight if possible. But screenwriting as it is practiced in the United States, and increasingly in other parts of the world, is definitely not the same as journalism, novel writing, non-fiction, or even writing for the stage. No screenplay exists on its own. Your script is part of an industry where thousands of other people make a living turning out products that amuse or terrify or outrage or gratify countless millions in a faceless mass audience. Alas, this industry isn't known as the *Screenwriters' Instructions-for-How-You-Should-Live-Your-Life* Business. It's called the *Entertainment* Business.

154

Scribble Exercise:

❑ What are your motivations for wanting to write?

❑ Why do you want to write screenplays instead of novels, or poems, or songs, or stage plays?

❑ If it were absolutely guaranteed that you would never make a single dime writing screenplays, would you still choose this discipline for self-expression?

❑ Do you like words, play word games, work crossword puzzles, collect expressive words? Do you enjoy teasing with the language?

❑ What kinds of books do you read? History? Biography? Novels? Classics or modern?

❑ Who are your favorite writers? Why?

CHAPTER NINE

THE BUSINESS OF SCREENWRITING

"Nobody knows anything."

— William Goldman

Regrettably, the most frequent question asked by new screenwriters isn't "How do I write a good script?" but "How do I break into the business?" The only legitimate answer is that everything you've ever heard about Hollywood is true. No matter what it is. That's the enigma.

THERE'S NO BUSINESS LIKE SHOW BUSINESS

Unlike most other industries where there are established procedures for entry-level jobs and recognized accomplishments that will get you promoted through to your retirement gold watch, there is no such structure in the Hollywood movie industry. To be more accurate, there are many, many structures — shifting, mercurial phantasms that look like doorways but aren't, and brick walls that are wide-open portals.

But make no mistake. Since its beginnings in the early years of this century when a few adventurous garment manufacturing entrepreneurs set themselves up in the new industry of moving photography, Hollywood's *raison d'être* has been to make a buck. Hollywood is a business, not an art. It is a giant factory where a collaborative operation of creative and financial forces comes together to turn out something that the public wants to see and is willing to pay money for. If you understand that rationale, you'll be way ahead of the busloads of starry-eyed hopefuls who arrive every day to test their luck at the roulette wheel of the movie industry.

Unlike many other creative endeavors, the process of making movies is a collaborative operation. As media observer Marshall McLuhan once said, "No one commits photography alone." In practical terms this means that the writer of a movie script is only one member of the team, and though the writer's words may serve as the foundation for the process, they're not necessarily going to be the same words by the time the process is finished.

In novel writing, the author is the sole creator. Even though the editor contributes to the creation of the book, as does the book jacket designer and the typesetter and the marketing department, what's on the pages between the covers is virtually one hundred percent the creation of the lone author. The book will stand or fall because of that author's creative vision translated to the printed page. Of course, if it's a Sidney Sheldon or Danielle Steele book, there will be a massive marketing and promotion effort by the publisher. Publishing no less than movies is a business. But when Sidney and Danielle go home at night to count their money, they know that the book on the shelves of the bookstore is their creation. For this reason, many writers are attracted to the novel as a form of expression. It is immensely satisfying to know that your efforts exist in the solid form of a book. You can put it on the coffee table, point to it with pride, and say, "That's mine. I did it."

The playwright, likewise, is the sole creator of his or her product. Of course, to be complete, a play must be put on the stage. There are actors and directors and set and costume designers and many, many other people who will contribute to the ultimate success or failure of a Broadway play. Nevertheless, the script itself is usually the product of a single writer, and there is an honored tradition in the live theater that not one word of the script will be altered in any way without the approval of that playwright.

This honored tradition simply does not exist in the movie business. The playwright does not sell his work to a live stage producer; he licenses its use, and he retains full creative rights to his material. When a screenwriter sells work to a movie producer, however, that work becomes the property of the producer. The producer owns the copyright and is legally deemed to be the author; that is, he can do anything he wants with the material.

Time Warner is introducing a new navigation system for its Full Service Network interactive video that will allow viewers to select movies by category and instantly link to different sites. For example, while watching a movie, pressing Link allows you to link to Pizza Hut so you can order a pizza and quickly resume watching your movie.

Imagine for a moment that you commission a distinguished portrait artist to paint a picture of your dog Sparky. After weeks of sketches and various poses, the artist designs a picture that captures the very essence of your pet. You pay the famous portrait artist his fee — and then you pick up the brush yourself and begin to daub splotches of pink fluorescent paint here and there on the canvas. Not satisfied with your additions, you hire a second painter to come in and retouch the famous artist's work. There's something not quite right, you tell the second painter. Sparky should be doing something rather than just staring out from the canvas.

The second artist lays down a new coat of white paint over the entire portrait — except for the famous painter's signature in the bottom right corner, and then proceeds to paint a series of comic-strip panels depicting Sparky at play, Sparky eating, Sparky napping, Sparky palling around with the neighborhood dogs, and Sparky doing his business in the back yard. Wonderful, you say, and you pay the second artist his fee.

Still, there's something missing, you feel, from this picture, so you hire a third painter to come in and fix things. You like the comic-book panels, you say, but somehow they don't fully capture the essential Sparkiness you had in mind. The third artist knows exactly what to do, and promptly cuts a hole in the middle of the portrait with scissors. He then makes a plaster cast of Sparky's head and inserts it into the hole, paints the plaster cast with grape jelly, and places a starched clown collar around the neck of the bust.

Now you have yourself a genuinely unique depiction of Sparky — and, best of all, it's a valuable signed original by the famous portrait painter!

This series of events would be absurd in the world of serious portrait painting. It is not so far-fetched in the world of moviemaking. Of course, no one deliberately sets out to make a bad movie, much less to turn a finely crafted work of art into a piece of junk. But movies are a process in a collaborative medium, and that means that more people, sometimes many more, than the original screenwriter are going to have a say in the ultimate look and feel of the movie product.

THE SCREENPLAY MARKET

You have written a *selling script*. Now you have to take off your creative hat and step into the business of selling your script to the other players in the collaborative medium: the producer, the director, the stars, and the public.

The Producer: Many people in movies go by the title of Producer, but let's define "producer" here as the person or entity such as a studio that has the power to get the movie made, that is, who puts up the money or causes the money to be raised that will pay you for your script and all the production people for their skills and efforts in making and marketing the movie. Even a very low-budget studio theatrical feature film will have a budget of ten to twenty million dollars, and, of course, the raw fiscal tonnage of *Titanic* has skewed the financing statistics out of all proportion. But no one in their right mind is going to risk any amount of money, certainly not hundreds of millions of dollars, unless they believe they have a reasonable chance of not only getting their money back, but also making a few dollars profit. Consequently, when producers buy a script, they want to be as certain as possible at this initial stage that the material they've bought will be successful.

Naturally, if anyone knew for sure what would be successful, there would be no risk, and the movie business would be very different indeed. But for all the computer projections, audience test marketing, and psychic divining, no one knows what's going to be a hit with the public at any given time. In the first place, it takes a minimum of one year, and more likely two years, before a movie can complete the trip from script to screen. In that time, the public's taste and interest can change greatly, so it doesn't do any good to imitate what's hot today. Producers take a huge gamble with their money or their investors' money that a particular script will somehow capture the public's imagination as a completed film two years from now. It's a scary prospect at best, and the men and women who function as Hollywood's major producers are risking their careers and their fortunes on their best guesses.

Understandably, they'd like to take as much of the risk as possible out of the guesswork, and they begin that process with the script. They look at themes and stories that have been popular with the public in the past, and they try to theorize on what might work in the future. Sometimes, this theorizing leads them to second-guess their own instincts. The same script they had faith in yesterday may not look so sure the morning after the producer learns that a similar project is in the works at another studio. Current events can change a fickle public's whim in an instant, and a script built on the hot trend of the moment may be cold and clammy by this afternoon. So a producer is constantly looking to get the script "right." Very often this means bringing in new writers with a fresh approach to rewrite the material according to what the producers believe the public will want to see.

161

Sometimes pictures go through a dozen or more rewrites by as many different writers before the producer settles on a version he or she is reasonably comfortable with.

The Director: Usually the first person hired after a script has been settled on is the director. The director is responsible for guiding the project from its beginnings on the page to its premiere showing on the screen. It is an unbelievably demanding job that requires stamina, talent, and no small amount of ego to successfully complete. Theatrical feature film has been described as a director's medium because, more than any other single person, the director must shape the film product into a commodity for public consumption. Of course, directors are interested in turning out an artistic success, but their reputation in the business and their future employment are dependent much more on whether or not they produce an economic success. If a director fails to maintain control of the picture's costs as well as its creative elements, the producers and financiers are less likely to bankroll the director's next project.

So a director is especially concerned with keeping a tight monopoly over all the circumstances of the filmmaking process — and that domination begins with the script. Even after the producers have approved a screenplay, directors are likely to want changes in the script for their own reasons. They may even bring in their own writers, people they've worked with successfully on previous projects, to shape the script in a special way. Most directors try to develop a distinctive style in their filmmaking. They're known for directing action-adventure films, or comedies, or romantic love stories, and in fact that reputation is usually so strong that the director will have a difficult time switching to another kind of film. Naturally, directors look for those elements in a script that are appropriate to their style, and they emphasize those elements in any screenplay they develop.

The Stars: Hollywood is and always has been a star-driven industry. Every actor in the business wants to be a star, and they're all looking

162

for just the right role in just the right script that will boost their career into the star category.

Those actors who do achieve real stardom look for certain kinds of material in screenplays. The public may not know the name of a director, and almost certainly will not know one screenwriter from another, but they will know what actors and actresses they like to watch. To some extent, an audience knows what to expect from a film starring Clint Eastwood or Kevin Costner or Julia Roberts or Meryl Streep, and those actors spend a great deal of effort and money cultivating their image with the public. As a consequence, some stars are recognized by the producers and financiers of movies as being bankable, that is, a film starring someone with such a high audience identification will probably do better at the box office than a film featuring a lesser known or less popular actor. Obviously this isn't always the case, as many disastrous films with major stars will testify, but by and large, the bigger the star, the better chance of success the picture will have.

The screenwriter would do well to keep in mind what this star power means. You are writing for stars and *potential stars*. On a practical level it means that actors love to meddle in scripts. A star can and will ask for a rewrite of a script to tailor it to a particular image. A lesser actor will beg a director to change a line or a bit of action so he can get a little more screen time or a better camera angle — and if that means changing the script, then so be it.

The Public: The movie industry is a business driven by the demands of a public just like the automobile business or the clothing business. It is this *mass audience* that is your toughest sell. You have no idea who they are, where they come from, or what they want. They are not your friends and family, and yet they respond to the same emotions. They do not have your experiences, and yet they respond to the universal human experience. They can be analyzed and studied, broken down by mathematical model, sociology, income, education, geogra phy, and test audience response, and yet you still will not know who they are. You can stand in line at your local multiplex theater with them, listen to them laugh and cry in the audience, and you still won't know. Only two things are certain about this mass audience:

✓ **They are not you.**

✓ **They are you.**

And this is where the writer's earned instinct comes in. No end of people in Hollywood will tell you they know how the audience will respond. Remember William Goldman's maxim — *Nobody knows anything*! You have to use your own instincts as a writer to connect with those people out there in the dark.

These four entities — producers, directors, stars, and the audience — are the deciding factors on whether a screenplay becomes a movie. And, not surprisingly, they all want exactly the same thing — a good story. Of course, that's easier said than done, but there are some very basic guidelines you should consider in writing and marketing your first screenplay:

1. **Is there one indisputable main character?** Remember that you are writing for stars, and stars do not like to share their screen time. More important, the audience needs to be able to identify with one character that will carry them through the story.

2. **Does the main character have a clearly defined problem to solve?** Remember the conflict focus. What is the main character's external goal? Why does the audience care about the outcome of the story?

3. **Is there distinct opposition to the main character focused in an antagonist?** Remember the moral dimension

164

of the dramatic conflict. How does the main character's battle affect the audience? If the main character loses, how will the antagonist's victory affect the audience?

4. Does the resolution of the problem require that the main character take *action* against the antagonist? Does your main character have a compelling need to act? Is there a time limit during which the character must take action or lose the battle by default?

5. Does the resolution of the problem bring the main character's *values* into question? Remember the character's internal need that will be exposed by the dramatic conflict. How will the audience know that the main character ends the drama as a changed person?

6. Are the principal dynamics of the story emotional rather than intellectual? Remember that movies play to our hearts, not our brains. As much as writers have social and political purposes, we are also in the business of entertaining the audience, of telling them a fascinating *story* rather than an obligatory lesson.

Of course you can find exceptions to all of these specifications, but if you will keep these six criteria resolutely in mind, you will produce a screenplay, no matter what the genre, that will be marketable to the greatest number of producers in the industry. Later, after you have written and sold a couple of successful films, you will be more free to experiment with radical arabesques of style and content.

BIG INDUSTRY, SMALL BUSINESS

Before *Titanic*, the average cost of producing and marketing a studio theatrical feature was about sixty million dollars. The vast amount of money put into a feature film means that the people who run the movie business aren't so much creative, artistic individuals as they are money people. Think of them as bankers, salespeople, and merchants, whose product happens to be entertainment rather than steel or rubber or concrete, and you'll have a much clearer picture of who you're dealing with as a screenwriter. As bankers, they're interested in the bottom line, a good return on their capital investment. As salespeople, they're interested in generating heat and creating a demand for their products. As merchants, they're interested in making a deal and moving their inventory. In fact, it's often been said in the movie business that it's not so much the movie a producer *wants* to make as the movie he *can* make; that is, the deal he can put together with the right script, director, and stars that will convince the bankers to finance his product and the marketers to get out and sell it.

Time Warner's corporate annual report announces, "Brands build libraries, libraries build networks, networks build distribution, distribution builds brands."

The big Hollywood studios that have vast production lots with soundstages and property departments and standing sets and location ranches where much of the production of movie product takes place are referred to as the majors. But the majors are more than just big tracts of real estate. They are huge international empires that control the movie product from its inception as an idea to its distribution in the neighborhood theater and right down to the actual celluloid print that's projected onto the screen. Even more, they are banks, financial institutions that invest or collect the investment for the movies they produce.

Exhibitors Cineplex Odeon is forming a joint venture with Sega GameWorks to develop "entertainment centers" featuring theaters, video arcades, restaurants, and retail outlets.

The major studios in Hollywood include Paramount, Universal, Fox, Sony Pictures/Columbia, Warner Brothers, Disney/Touchstone, MGM/UA, and SKG DreamWorks. In turn, each of these major studios has a number of minor branches dedicated to particular genres or budgets of film, and they have distribution deals with independent producers as well as cofinancing deals with other major studios. Together, they make the monoliths of the old studio-system heyday look like mom-and-pop corner stores. Today's major studio is not in the movie business. It is a mega-hyper-circumglomerate revenue harvest mechanism, composed of an intricate tangle of global alliances for acquisition, financing, production, sales, and distribution for everything from designer parasols to ambrosial edibles.

On the other side of the desk, there's you.

Before you finished the screenplay, you were a creative artist. Now, you are a businessperson. You are in the screenwriting *business*. Your goal is to sell your screenplay for as much money as you can. With any luck, your screenplay will be made into a movie and you will get more money in the form of a production bonus. The movie will be a hit, and you will have the opportunity to write more screenplays. Your price will rise and you will be able to demand more money. That is the business you are in. Instead of selling vacuum cleaners or automobiles or insurance, your inventory consists of movie scripts for sale.

"No writer is ever going to get his hands on a percentage of my revenues."

— Lew Wasserman, Chairman of MCA (Universal)

Your customer is the studio executive, a Suit, in Hollywood language, sitting on the other side of the desk. The Suit has always been on the opposite side of the table, and will hold dominion there until the end of time. That is the reality of the movie business. The Suit's single, overriding question will always be, "How much?"

If you can treat being a screenwriter as you would any other business, then there are some agencies and people who may be able to help you become successful.

THE WRITERS GUILD OF AMERICA

Writers by their nature tend to be introspective. We're highly individualistic and usually prefer to work alone. So it may seem strange that almost all screenwriters in Hollywood belong to an organization that is the antithesis of individualism — a labor union. The Writers Guild of America is just that, a union officially certified by the National Labor Relations Board just like the United Auto Workers. Well, maybe not quite like that, because while the UAW members generally work on an assembly line as part of a team, and frequently do the same repetitive job day in and day out, writers for the most part can still set their own hours and working conditions and negotiate for their own individual pay. But it hasn't always been that way in the movie industry, and that's why the Writers Guild came into being.

"Writers are the most important people in the business, and we must never let them find that out."

—Irving Thalberg

In the early days of Hollywood when the industry was controlled by the studio moguls like Louis B. Mayer and the Warner brothers, writers worked in conditions not unlike those of the auto worker on the assembly line. The studio system churned out pictures at a prodigious rate, and writers sat in offices on the studio lots devising scripts for those pictures. Sometimes they wrote whole scripts, sometimes only scenes, sometimes revisions of revisions of scenes. Writers were employees of the studios and nothing more. There is even the famous, perhaps apocryphal, story of the day Louis B. Mayer walked into the writers' building on the MGM lot. After a moment of listening to the silence, Mr. Mayer screamed, "I'm paying you to write, and I don't hear no writing going on!" At which instant, a dozen type-writers began to clatter — until Mayer left the building.

Nowhere was this attitude toward writers as expendable employees more insidious than in the matter of screen credits. As employees, writers had no say in the way their work was used, or even in whether they received credit for their work. In short, they were regarded not as creative contributors to the process of moviemaking, but as humanoids who somehow managed to fill blank pages with words. Screen credit was assigned by the studio, and the stories of abuse are legion. Often credit was given to a producer, or a producer's friend, or a producer's son who may have had little or nothing to do with the creation of the script.

In 1933, a special meeting of the Screen Writers' Guild of the Authors League of America took place in Hollywood and the fledgling organi-zation took the first steps to become what is now the Writers Guild of America, a labor union that represents screen, television, and radio writers for the purpose of collective bargaining with the motion pic-ture producers and broadcast networks. Known as the Producers Guild, or collectively as "the companies," these studios and networks have agreed to a master contract with the Writers Guild called the *Minimum Basic Agreement*, or *MBA*. This master contract establishes minimum rates of pay for certain kinds of writing, and sets up partic-ular working conditions for writers in the industry. The MBA is rene-gotiated every few years just as any other labor contract, and every few years, it seems, the Writers Guild goes out on strike. Our last strike in 1988 lasted over five and a half months. Since then, the contract has been successfully renewed without any work stoppage. For all the truth of writers being individual creative beings, in the business of screenwriting we are part entrepreneur and part hired hand, and sometimes the only protection we have from mistreatment in the industry is the Writers Guild.

You do not have to be a member of the WGA to sell a script, but when you do sell an original piece of material, you will be eligible to join the Guild and receive the protections of membership.

Meanwhile, there are some services of the Guild you can use without being a member. One of the most important is the WGA's Intellectual Property Registry. The Registration Department was set up to help establish a writer's completion date for literary material written for theatrical motion pictures, television, and radio. Registration is not the same as a copyright, but it is a testimony to the existence of a script at a certain time. This kind of evidence may be useful in certain situations where there is a dispute about the authorship of material and possible legal action.

THEY STOLE MY IDEA!

Before we go any further, let's try to clear up some misconceptions about what kinds of literary material can and cannot be protected. The field of intellectual property rights is complicated, so you should always consult a competent attorney if you suspect you have a problem. But before you spend two to three hundred dollars an hour for an attorney, let's look at the situation in broad terms.

There is no question that theft occurs in Hollywood. Ideas, scripts, characters, and concepts are stolen all the time. No doubt you've heard of some of the famous cases. But the fact is that literary theft is far less of a problem than many writers would like to believe; and it is extremely difficult to prove even if it does occur. The most often heard lament from a writer is that *such and such a producer stole my idea.* Now it is unfortunate if true, and certainly less than ethical behavior on the part of the producer. However, the hard fact is that you cannot protect an idea. The general idea or outline for a script cannot be copyrighted. Nothing prohibits two people from coming up with the same idea concurrently. Perhaps the most famous case in history of

170

idea simultaneity is that of **Charles Darwin** and **Alfred Russel Wallace**. In 1858 they each independently developed the theory of natural selection. Darwin's *The Origin of Species* was published first, and today we don't call the theory of evolution Wallaceism.

Hardly a week goes by in Hollywood that someone doesn't claim that a movie or television show was really their idea that the producer stole. Still, the truth is that an author's idea cannot be protected, only the dramatic expression of that author's idea. In practical terms, this means that your specific dialogue and story line may be protected from theft; however, you should not be surprised if someone else comes up with a very similar story based on a very similar premise and containing very similar characters. After all, we're all exposed to the same events and thoughts floating around in the world, and the law of averages says that more than one of us are going to come up with the same idea at the same time.

Your best protection, then, is to register your completed screenplay with the WGA Registration Department. You take or send one copy of your screenplay to the Guild, following the WGA Registration Department guidelines, and pay $20. You will get a receipt verifying that on a certain day you deposited a copy of your script with the Guild. If, subsequent to that date, you give your screenplay to a producer to read and that producer rejects it, but in a year or two you see a movie on the screen produced by that same company and using specific material from your screenplay, then you may have a case to take to court. If so, you should consult a knowledgeable litigation attorney.

Don't be in too big of a rush to condemn the producer, however. The fact is, it is rare that such outright and audacious theft will occur. It is much more likely that there will be some resemblance between the finished film and many drafts of the script by different writers. Some of those similarities may seem to be to your script. However, keep in mind that once a writer chooses a topic and begins to make choices to develop a plot, it is inevitable that there will be similarities to the work of other writers who have chosen the same topic and developed a comparable plot. If the essential story is, for instance, about the arrival on earth of an extraterrestrial who is befriended by a young boy, then certain scenes, events, and even characters will unavoidably be nearly alike in content no matter what two versions of the script are compared.

In addition to registering a copy of your screenplay with the WGA, your best protection is to keep a clear paper trail of all contact you have with any producers who are reviewing your script. Keep a log of all your telephone calls and copies of all correspondence. Verify your meetings with a follow-up thank-you note that mentions the title and subject of your discussions. But above all, do not be paranoid! Paranoia leads to defensiveness and sometimes antagonism, and no producer wants to do business with somebody who walks in the door reeking of suspicion. Remember that the movie business is complex and many, many writers develop similar stories and even similar characters. Do the best job of writing that you can and you'll succeed much more surely than by screaming foul every time an idea that resembles yours appears on the screen.

TRUE-LIFE MEMOIRS

Some events of history — Lincoln's assassination, the Chicago fire, etc. — are in the public domain. That is, the facts are known and are available to any and all writers. The closer in time an event is to the present day, however, the more problematic it becomes. While an event such as a sensational trial may be public domain because it's in all the newspapers, you may not have the freedom to use that information as you see fit.

Public figures have rights, as do their heirs and estates, and you cannot freely make up stories about them without the risk of libel. This is especially true of people who are not in the public eye. Their right to privacy is important, and you do not have the right to tell their story without their specific permission.

Your best course of action if you are considering writing a story about a real person is to consult an attorney and draw up a *Life Option Contract* in which your subject gives you permission to tell his or her story before you begin writing. By the way, don't assume that just because the person you're writing about is your sister or your uncle that you have automatic permission. Even the best of families can become nasty when money is involved.

> "*I loathe writing. On the other hand I'm a great believer in money.*"
>
> — S.J. Perelman

U.S. COPYRIGHT

In addition to recording your script with the WGA, you may want to go the extra step of registering the copyright with the U.S. Copyright Office. According to the Copyright Act, copyright automatically exists from the moment the work is created in a fixed form, so no registration or other action is required to secure your ownership of a piece of material. However, there are some advantages to actually registering your copyright with the Copyright Office. The most significant of these is that if you must go to court in an infringement suit, the registration of a copyright allows you to sue for statutory damages and attorney's fees. Otherwise, the courts may only allow you actual damages.

To register the copyright of your screenplay, you must send two copies of the script, a filing fee of $20, and *Application Form PA*, which you can obtain by calling (202) 707-9100. On the title page of your script you should include the copyright symbol (©), the year of first publication, and your name. That's all there is to it. Now you're ready to show your screenplay to potential producers!

YOUR TEAM

There are three people who may be able to help you get your screenplay read by the right producer: a *literary agent*, an *entertainment attorney*, and a *personal manager*.

Contrary to popular belief, you do not have to have an agent to get your script read. But it helps. At best, an agent is your mentor and guide through the maze of Hollywood. At worst, an agent is a necessary evil. But let's clear up a few misconceptions about what an agent is and is not.

✓ **An agent is not an employment office**. True, the agent's job is to get you work, but you can't expect the agent to keep you employed steadily. The agent functions as a kind of broker, matching writers with available projects and scripts with interested producers. An agent can only go so far in introducing you or your material to prospective buyers — but no one can sell a production company something they don't want. Even the word sell is probably misapplied to an agent because that makes it seem that selling scripts is no different from selling encyclopedias or ironing boards. The fact is that agents are not so much salespeople as they are advisors to both client and customer. If the customer wants to buy, the agent can match the producer with a client. If the customer is not inclined to buy, there's not much the agent can do. The truth is that perhaps one out of ten jobs you get as a writer will come as a direct result of the agent's efforts. Instead, *you* are the person who will sell. You have to make the contacts and network with industry people, then the agent can follow up to negotiate your contract.

✓ **An agent is not your mother**. It's not your agent's job to comfort you when you're feeling blue or talk you through your down periods. The agent won't lift your spirits by telling you how fantastic you are, and there will almost never be cookies and milk waiting for you after a hard day at the keyboard. The agent is a businessperson in a hard-nosed and sometimes brutal industry. The agent needs for you to be an adult, not a deadweight.

✓ **An agent is not a banker**. If your financial life is in a mess, don't expect the agent to bail you out, or even to get you that "one little job" so you can pay the rent. There are, of course, stories of those big-hearted agents who kept their clients' careers going by loaning them money and allowing them to live in the guest house until they hit the big time. Don't count on it. It's up to you to take care of your own economic well-being.

✓ **Agents are in business for themselves**. They have mortgages, and car payments, and kids in private school, and office staffs to support. An agent gets ten percent of the clients' fees for writing — but ten percent of the *working* clients' fees. If an agent has, let's say, fifty writers in the stable, at least half of those must be getting paid at any given time in order for the agent to make a living. The hard business truth is that it really doesn't make any difference to the agent whether the ten percent comes from you or the next writer on the list, as long as the agent can meet the monthly expenses.

✓ **An agent is your team member**. You have to trust the agent and the agent has to trust you, or you're both going to sink. Certainly an agent must like your work and believe in your abilities. But at the same time, you must have some faith in the agent's instincts. The agent is, after all, supposed to have an ear to the ground and should know what producers are looking for. If your agent says that a particular piece of your material just isn't going to sell in the current market, you need to listen. Rather than jumping immediately on the defensive and refusing to make any changes, try to work out with your agent some way of adjusting the material so that it can go on the market. Keep in mind that agents only make money if you make money, so they're just as eager as you are to make a sale.

175

✓ **The agent is the business half of your partnership.** In contract negotiations, the agent can keep you, the creative person, at a comfortable distance from the producer so that you're not faced with making both creative and financial decisions. As a writer you want to be cooperative and give the production company what they need to make a successful movie. But you need to limit that cooperation to the artistic arena or you might very well find yourself working for free. When the producer wants you to do an extra rewrite, or maybe another script on the side, you can always say the magic words, "Talk to my agent."

✓ **The agent supplies validity.** An agent's submission of a script to a producer testifies that the material is worthy of consideration. The producer is far more likely to read a script sent in by an agent than one that comes in over the transom. In fact, most production companies simply do not accept unsolicited material. They will often return the envelope unopened. In part this is because of the fear of lawsuits over copyright infringement, but it is also because the producers don't have time to read material that hasn't been screened by someone who believes it's right for them. Of course, you may meet a producer at a party, or live next door, or be recommended by someone the producer trusts, and therefore get the script to the company without an agent. But most of the time an agent is a necessary channel of communication from writer to producer.

GETTING YOUR OWN AGENT

The best way to go about getting an agent as a beginning screenwriter is to be recommended by a producer or by one of the agent's clients who has read your work and is willing to vouch for you. Even if you know someone who has an agent, however, asking a friend to testify on your behalf is not as simple as it sounds. No matter how it may appear to you, your friend probably isn't that secure about their relationship with producers and agents. It's a funny business that way, but everyone is always a little uncertain about their standing, so introducing a prospective client to an agent is risky. If you're a fabulous writer, your friend may be diminishing his own ranking with the agency; and if you're not such a good writer, the agent is going to have doubts about your friend's judgment.

Your first step in getting your own agent, then, is to consult the list of *Franchised Agencies* that is published by the Writers Guild. These are agencies that have agreed to abide by the Writers Guild MBA in their negotiations with signatory producers. Some of the agents on the list are huge mega-agencies like William Morris or Creative Artists Agency or International Creative Management, but most are medium to small agents. New writers have virtually no chance of being represented by the mega-agencies, who specialize in taking on clients *after* they have become a success. They package writers and directors and stars together to make movies — and all the elements of the package are represented by the same agency so the commissions are multiplied accordingly.

Among the medium and small agencies, some have reputations for dealing primarily in television, others in feature films, and some even in particular areas like television sit-coms or animation. You need to make yourself known to these agents so they can decide if they want to represent you.

Of course, the worst possible way to make yourself known is to send them an unsolicited script. Chances are you won't get a reply of any kind, and your script will find an instant home in the trash dumpster outside the agent's office. If you have no screenwriting credits and no one to introduce you, there's only one way to get to approach an agent — a query letter. Like a resume that gets you the job interview, a query letter is your best sales tool for attracting an agent.

Scribble Exercise:

Write a query letter to an agency requesting that they read your sample screenplay. Keep the letter as short and easy to read as possible.

❏ In the first paragraph, interest the agent in your story by providing a hook, a provocative statement about your story or an intriguing question about the main character. Give the agent a *very brief* summary of the premise of the story, such as, "a story about a young man who almost starts World War III by tapping into the national defense computer with his home PC."

❏ In the second paragraph, give the agent a little background about yourself. If you're a published writer in some other area such as journalism, be sure to say so, without necessarily giving a complete list of your credits. If you're a professional or expert in some field, be sure to mention that.

❏ Ask the agency if they would be interested in reading your screenplay and offer to express mail it to them. You may also want to include a self-addressed stamped postcard with the simple statement, "Yes, I am interested in reading your screenplay _____." typed neatly on the back.

If an agent does respond favorably to your query, send the script immediately with a polite cover letter. Then wait. Six to eight weeks is not an unreasonable amount of time to wait for a reply. If you have not heard from the agent in two months, you may want to send another polite reminder note or telephone call. If you still don't hear, assume that the agent is not interested in handling your material.

Of course you can send query letters to several agents at the same time, but avoid blanketing the whole list. Stick to two or three for the first time out, and if you don't receive a response from them, then go to the next two or three on your list. And remember, spelling, punctuation, and neatness do count! Give the agent the most professional picture of yourself that you possibly can.

Also remember, even if you are accepted by an agency, that having an agent is not the same thing as having a career. You are still going to have to hustle your material, network with contacts, and continue to produce scripts that your agent can market to potential producers. Your job isn't over, it's just begun.

One more word before we leave the subject of agents. No legitimate agent will ask you for a "reader's fee" or any money up front in order to consider your material. If you do get such a request, run as fast as possible in the opposite direction.

"Being a real writer means being able to do the work on a bad day."
— Norman Mailer

ENTERTAINMENT ATTORNEYS

Even if you have a very good agent, there's another member you want on your team, an *entertainment attorney*. Some entertainment attorneys are willing to function like agents, that is, sending out material and negotiating deals, but for the most part a good entertainment attorney is most useful in reviewing contracts for you. The agent negotiates the deal, sometimes in highly pressured situations, and hammers out the general outlines of the understanding you have with the producer. The producer will then have the legal staff or business affairs department draw up a contract for you to sign. Most agents are not lawyers, and though they may be very familiar with contract language, they generally have neither the time nor the temperament to look over the fine points of legal rhetoric. An attorney familiar with entertainment law can potentially save you thousands of dollars and untold anguish down the road by reviewing your contract now before you sign it. Most of these attorneys will work on a commission basis or an hourly fee of two to three hundred dollars. Be sure you have a clear agreement before your attorney begins work, but never hesitate to have any contract reviewed. The entertainment attorney's counsel is worth whatever the cost may be.

PERSONAL MANAGERS

One other member you may have on your screenplay sales team is a *personal manager*. Unlike agents, personal managers are not regulated by the Writers Guild, and while they technically cannot solicit work for a writer nor negotiate a contract, they can be useful in shaping the writer's career. Most managers take a fifteen percent cut of the writer's fees and provide services such as publicity, press releases, and general promotion for their clients. Actors have used personal managers for years, but writers have only recently started using them. Most writers find that the combination of an agent and a personal manager is overkill, and the relationship between the manager and agent can be one of conflict, leaving the writer trying to please two masters. Still, personal managers tend to be easier to come by than agents, and if you don't have an agent yet, a personal manager may be able to open some doors that you cannot open by yourself. Remember, though, that managers, like agents, only make money if their clients make money, so you're still going to have to do the lion's share of the hustling yourself.

THE PITCH

Now, put your screenplay in a drawer and don't look at it. Your next job has nothing to do with those 120 pieces of paper. Your next job isn't written, it's oral. You're going to pitch the idea of your screenplay to the studio Suit across the desk.

Pitching is a necessity in the film business, requiring you to reduce your screenplay to a couple of lines, explaining it in the fewest possible words with the greatest possible excitement.

It may seem strange, even unfair, that the profession of writing hinges so much on an oral presentation. But imagine that you've just seen a great movie and you're eager to share your experience with your friend; that is, you want your friend to have the same fun or excitement or emotional involvement that you did. Almost invariably you'll begin by saying, "I just saw this great movie ..." To which your friend will respond, "Yeah, what's it about?" That's your cue to give your friend the succinct story line that will make him want to see the movie. You rarely tell the entire story point-for-point, or describe the kind of cars the characters drive, or any of a thousand other details. You're more likely to say something like, "It's about this cop who's trapped alone in this building that's being taken over by these really evil terrorists." You've distilled the movie to the essence of the story, the hook, the central conflict that kept you engaged for two hours.

The audience itself depends on the pitch in one form or another to guide its choices. Cinema pundit bites are designed to hook you into the theater just as surely as the glossy trailers and one-sheet posters. Producers and studio executives are no different. They want to turn out material that will interest the audience more or less instantaneously. Of course, there are obvious drawbacks to this kind of thinking. Some of the best movies simply do not reduce to simple one- or two-sentence synopses. But beneath this obvious reason for the pitch, there are some fundamental business and aesthetic reasons why writing is often sold by mouth rather than by eye.

1. The entertainment business moves fast. Like retail sales, it depends on capturing the imagination of an audience and riding the cutting edge of popular consciousness. Studio executives listen to perhaps fifty to a hundred formal pitches a week, not to mention the informal story pitches that come at parties, tennis games, the auto repair shop, and restaurants. There simply isn't time to read that many scripts, and many of the ideas producers hear will be the same or nearly the same. There has to be some efficient way of sorting them out, and the oral pitch has evolved as that device. In a few minutes an executive or producer can determine if the story idea is something the company wants to pursue. If the pitch is enticing, the executive may ask to read the script.

2. There is also a fundamental aesthetic reason for the simplicity of the pitch. Film is much more like oral communication than written communication. Although the screenplay is a form of written literature, the ultimate product it is designed to serve is not literature in the strictest sense. With books or poetry we have the luxury of time. We can read and reread a passage to understand its meaning or to savor its style. That simply isn't possible in movies. Certainly you can watch a movie over and over again on tape, but that's not how it's designed to be seen. Like oral communication, movies exist in linear time. You have to understand what's happening more or less immediately. This is not to say that there cannot be deliberate ambiguities in plot, but that the plot itself must move with such deftness that the audience trusts those complexities will be resolved in due course. We are carried along by the unfolding energy of the film just as we once were transported by the ancient troubadours and storytellers around the fire. The cinematic form speaks much more to that dynamic experience of storytelling than to the meditative experience of reading.

3. While it is true that producers and executives are looking for projects they like, it is equally true that they are looking for writers they like. Like a job interview, they're looking for those ineffable qualities in a writer that will allow them to do business comfortably. This is an industry of insecurities and intuitions about relationships. The producer has to be able to trust the writer, to trust the writer's instincts, to trust the writer's reliability, to trust the writer's enthusiasm. No one in this business says *yes* easily. In fact, in a very real sense it is a business that is built on saying *no*. *No* is safe. *No* doesn't risk a job or a career or millions of dollars. So everything you can do to help the producer say *yes* is in your favor.

Putting together a good pitch is more than telling the story; it's capturing the gist of the plot together with the essence of the emotion that the plot evokes in the audience. Think of the pitch as a kind of commercial that you're going to use to sell your product, your screenplay. Every writer has a style of pitching. Some like to draw word pictures, others literally bound around the room acting out scenes. Some have even been known to tape-record their pitches and play them on video- or audiotape so that the producer is thrust into the viewing audience mode immediately.

Scribble Exercise:

Compose a pitch for your screenplay, and practice it aloud.

❑ Create a mood. Locate your listener in the special world where your story takes place.

❑ Nail down the main character clearly. Do not spend time on long physical descriptions, but give your listener the core of the character metaphorically.

❑ Capture the basic conflict the character faces. What is the question that's posed to the audience within the first ten minutes of the film?

❑ Develop a hook line. Think about what would make *you* want to see this movie. The story is told that Gene Roddenberry sold the original *Star Trek* series with the hook line "Wagon Train in Space."

In the face-to-face meeting itself, remember that you want to be the star of the show, but at the same time, you want the producers or executives to feel that they have a stake in the success of your story. Perhaps the best way to accomplish this is to make sure you get the producers involved in the telling. Get them talking and contributing to your story as you go along. Don't read your pitch — talk it. Likewise, don't have your pitch so memorized that you can't respond to comments or break your concentration without starting over again from the top. Keep your enthusiasm high, but make sure you also keep watch on the producers' attention. If their eyes start to glaze over, be prepared to shift your emphasis. And, if you're working with a partner, both of you should contribute to the pitch, like sports announcers with one doing the play-by-play and the other doing the color commentary. Above all, keep your pitch short. Time in the movie business literally is money.

COVERAGE

If the Suit likes your pitch, you'll know right away. He'll ask to read your script. At that point you can either have a copy of the script with you or, better yet, have your agent forward a copy of the script under agency letterhead. Unfortunately, a producer agreeing to read your script does not mean that he's going to read it himself. Every studio, producer, and star in the business employs someone else to read for them. That's right, the people who make the decisions rarely read the material themselves, at least in the initial phase of decision making. Instead there are readers or story analysts who are paid to read your script and prepare a digest of the basic plot and characters. It's called *coverage* and every script in the business is subjected to it. Like pitching, coverage is a fact of the business dictated largely by time. The story analysts read scripts, novels, treatments, and galley proofs of novels soon to be published looking for good movie material. They write one- to two-page summaries of the material and evaluate it according to basic idea, characters, writing style, and budget — and it's these compact summaries of the material that the producer is most likely to read rather than the scripts themselves.

185

There's a lot of complaining among Hollywood writers about this system of readers reading scripts and passing along their digests to the producers, but for the most part the readers are intelligent, perceptive professionals who read thousands of submissions and know how to cull the good material from the mediocre. Sometimes, when the coverage is favorable, several readers or development executives will review the script before it is passed to the higher-level producers and executives, and every reader who contributes a recommendation adds that much more credibility to your script. Eventually, scripts reach the decision-making level, and because enough people have read and approved of the material, by the time the top executive reads it he or she is already favorably disposed. That doesn't guarantee that your script will be produced, but it does testify that it's been recognized as worthy of production — and that the writer is worthy of recognition.

MAKING DEALS

So after you've met with the producer, the readers have covered your script, and the studio executives like it, is it time to accept your Academy Award yet? Not quite. Although it's certainly possible that a producer or studio will buy your screenplay outright, that's not the most likely way things will happen.

If there is anything true of Hollywood, it's that there is no one standard, predictable way for a writer to get material sold and on the screen. Much depends on just where and how the project was initiated: directly for a studio or network, with an independent producer, with a star, or a myriad of other ways scripts get produced. The facts are that every year the Writers Guild Registration Department accepts over forty thousand scripts and treatments, but each year Hollywood produces and releases only about three hundred feature films. A small handful of these feature films are commercial successes.

With the understanding that there is no single way for a script to become a movie, let's look at what may be the most common scenario.

186

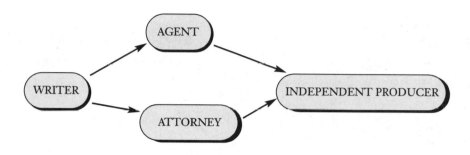

Via your agent, your attorney, or sometimes yourself, your script finds its way to an independent production company. This may be a major independent or simply a producer in a small office. The producer likes your script.

THE OPTION AGREEMENT — DEAL MEMO

The independent producer will, in all likelihood, not buy the script outright, but will offer to option the material from you, that is, he will promise to buy it if certain conditions are met during a specified period of time. In exchange for the promise, during that time the producer has the exclusive right to try to use his influence and reputation to obtain financing for the film. He may attach a star or a director to the project to increase its attractiveness, or he may try to secure partial financing from several sources.

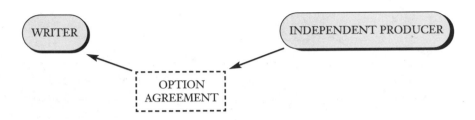

The option fee should be ten percent of the agreed-upon purchase price, but the actual amount is negotiable. During the option period, the writer is specifically prohibited from doing anything with the script, but once the option expires, all rights revert to the writer, and the writer retains any option payments that have been made during the course of the agreement.

You will naturally be tempted to sign the simple option agreement and let the producer get on with the job of selling your script to a studio. However, no matter how seductive it may be to sign on the dotted line at this stage, *do not do it!*

1. Consult with your agent or, if you do not have an agent, with a good entertainment attorney first. The option agreement is the *only* piece of paper you will ever have to establish your rights in the deal. Although there is a commonly used phrase in options to the effect that *this agreement is in contemplation of a full contract to be executed at a later date*, such a contract is a studio-level document that requires six Suits to transport and three tiers of archangels to interpret. You will never be in the presence of this esteemed covenant.

2. It is extremely important that you insert the exact wording "For purposes of this contract, Writer shall be deemed a '*professional writer*' pursuant to the Writers Guild of America Minimum Basic Agreement" into your option agreement. This simple phrase will entitle you to the protections of the WGA Minimum Basic Agreement even if you are not yet a member of the Writers Guild.

GOING TO THE BANK

Sooner or later, the independent producer will have to line up with other producers at the teller's window of one of the major studios for significant capital and distribution.

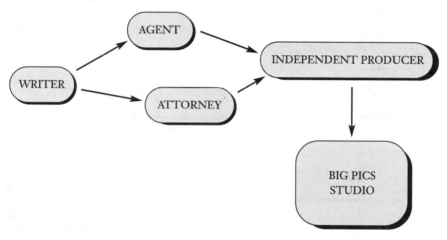

The studio, of course, will have certain requirements for the film just as a bank has requirements for a loan. They may want a particular director or stars for the project, and they will almost certainly want the script rewritten. At that point, the script may be put into development. The term *development* can mean many different things, but at base it means that you or someone else will be rewriting the material to please executives, stars, directors, and financiers before the project receives a green light. Ideally, the studio has given the producer a certain amount of development money, and he in turn will commission a rewrite from you.

However, there is always the possibility at this point that the studio will like the project, but will want to hire a more experienced, name writer to rework the material. If so, depending on the provisions of your option contract, you may be paid the purchase price for your script and then be off the project. It is also possible that you may still be part of the process, either as a writer or in some other capacity, and it is possible that you will not be paid for the script until a time in the future. It is very common, for instance, that the original writer is not paid for the script until commencement of principal photography, in other words, the day the movie actually goes before the cameras. In the meantime your option will be renewed as necessary and you will receive regular option payments.

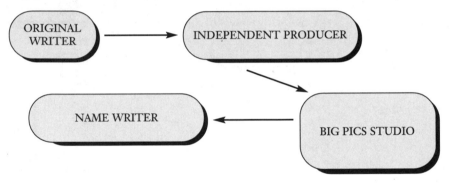

As you may have gathered from this scenario, it is quite possible that after you have optioned your script, you may not have the opportunity to do any more work on it beyond the first rewrite. The issue arises, then, of who gets credit on the screen if more than one writer has contributed to the shooting script.

SCREEN CREDIT

Regardless of whether or not you are a member of the Writers Guild, screen credit for writing is always determined solely by the Writers Guild of America in a process called ***arbitration***. When a movie nears completion, the production company submits a *Notice of Tentative Credits* to the WGA, listing what they believe should be the writing credits. The company also submits a copy of each draft of the script from the original optioned material through all versions to the shooting script. If more than one writer or more than one writing team has contributed to the screenplay, the Guild establishes a committee of writers to assign credit.

The Credit Arbitration committee members, acting independently of each other and without knowing the names of the writers involved, read all of the versions of the script to determine what writers contributed to what degree to the final version of the film. It is an extremely difficult and demanding task because a writer's reputation in the industry is built on screen credits. The committee members, therefore, are meticulous in their examinations. As a general rule, for a second writer to receive credit, the contribution must consist of more than fifty percent of the dramatic construction, original and different sequences, original characterizations, and dialogue. There have been instances in which every line of dialogue has been changed and still the committee can find no significant change in the screenplay as a whole. Conversely, there have been instances in which a change in one portion of a script is so significant that the entire screenplay is affected.

For the most part, screen credit will take one or a combination of four forms:

✓ **Written by**, When a writer has created both the story and screenplay; that is, the entire work is wholly original and no other writer has contributed to the final form of the shooting script.

✓ **Story by**, when a writer contributes the story and no other source material, such as earlier drafts of the screenplay or a novel, is involved, but that writer does not write the ultimate version of the script.

✓ **Screen Story by**, if a writer is furnished with some source material, such as a newspaper or magazine article, but takes from it only a broad, general idea or incident.

✓ **Screenplay by**, when the writer has written the final script, but that script is based on earlier material, such as an original screenplay by another writer.

When two writers write as a team, they are regarded as one entity for the sake of credit. Therefore the credit

Written by
George & Martha

means that George and Martha worked together as a team. However, the screen credit

Written by
George and Martha

means that George and Martha were judged by the arbitration committee to have each contributed equally to the final shooting draft of the screenplay, but they did not work together as a team.

192

The permutations are nearly limitless, which is why credit determination is confusing and frequently painful for all concerned. However, if you write a wholly original screenplay, you can be certain that the very least you will receive under Writers Guild arbitration guidelines is shared *Story by* credit.

Another certainty is that your screenplay will be rewritten, either by you or by other writers. Rewriting is a fact of life in the movie business. It happens to all writers. Sometimes the reasons for rewriting a screenplay are capricious; at other times there will be very good grounds for making changes. The process can be frustrating for the writer of an original screenplay, and those frustrations give rise to another major concern of screenwriters in Hollywood — creative rights.

CREATIVE RIGHTS

Historically, the profession of screenwriting has had a very different evolution from that of other literary forms. Because the writing of the script is only part of the complete procedure of making a film, the words on the page of a screenplay are not regarded with the same reverence as they might be in legitimate theater or novel writing. The issue is, in a collaborative medium, just how much creative input should the screenwriter have?

The 1988 Minimum Basic Agreement contract between the Writers Guild and the production companies addresses this concern by establishing some fundamental rights that screenwriters have. The intent of these provisions is that the writer be routinely included for script changes and consultations throughout the pre-production, production, post-production, and marketing of a film. The MBA is very complex, but the creative rights established for screenwriters apply mostly to original feature film and television scripts that are more than ninety minutes in length. Some of the more important provisions are:

1. A company may not disseminate critiques or synopses of any literary material that it has not optioned to anyone outside the company without the writer's consent. In spite of this regulation, it is a very common practice for production companies to share "coverage." The difficulty is that a script you submit to Universal Studios, for instance, may have already been rejected by Fox Studios, and rather than reading your script, the Universal executives simply read the unfavorable synopsis that was prepared by Fox.

2. The writer may restrict the extent to which a company may shop the writer's material to third parties. Everyone wants to think they're the first to see your script, so you will want to limit the number of studios or other companies a producer can take your material to. Otherwise you could find that people have read your script and rejected it even before you've had a chance to meet with them.

3. The writer of an original screenplay is entitled to perform the first rewrite. Once producers have optioned or purchased your material, they normally have the right to do anything they want to change that material. This provision means that you get the first opportunity to satisfy the producer's requested changes.

4. The producer or creative executive is required to consult with the writer to discuss each set of revisions the company requests. This rule is intended to prevent the company from simply sending the writer notes with no explanation and no opportunity for discussion.

5. The writer is entitled to meaningful discussion of the translation of his or her vision to the screen, including all aspects of the movie's tone, location, casting, and so forth.

6. The producer will arrange a meeting between the writer and the director to discuss how they can best work together.

7. **If a writer is required by the company to travel in connection with work on a project, then the company is required to provide first class travel, board, and lodging.** This does not mean that the writer will necessarily be required to travel, only that if he or she is, the production company must pay the expenses.

8. **The company must invite all participating writers to view a cut of the film prior to the final cut and in sufficient time to implement the writer's editing suggestions.** They don't have to take your suggestions, but they are supposed to give you the opportunity to make them.

9. **Credited writers must be invited to the first sneak preview, if any, held in Los Angeles County.**

10. **Credited writers must be furnished with a videocassette of the movie.**

Wait a minute. Doesn't all of this sound like ordinary professional courtesy? Yes, you'd think so. But as you can see, screenwriters are not shown the degree of respect we have earned. You may also have realized by now that in order to get that respect, we have to be particularly vigilant about our written and verbal agreements with producers and studios.

"No man but a blockhead ever wrote, except for money."
— Samuel Johnson

HOW MUCH?

Most contracts customarily offer writers five percent, or five points, of the producer's *net profits* in a theatrical motion picture. This sounds pretty good until you start trying to define exactly what *net profits* are.

Disputes tend to arise not over the amount of money to be paid for a script, which is reasonably simple to determine, but over the *back end*, that is, the money and other provisions that are agreed upon beyond the actual payment for the script.

Creative accounting is the term that's often applied to the way movie studios define where their money comes from. The truth is that most theatrical films are not very profitable at all. Oh, all the participants get paid, and the chances are that the movie will make some money over the long run from video release, and television, and foreign rights, but very few films are so overwhelmingly successful that their profits are clear. Even if the film does not make a profit, however, a few happy participants like big-name star actors, producers, and directors who have a gross participation still make money. Gross revenues are a pretty straightforward accounting of how much money a movie takes in at the box office, less the amounts that are deducted for the exhibitor and distributor. There are various kinds of gross participation, but let's just say that if anyone ever offers you *gross points*, snap it up immediately. Chances are, you're going to be offered *net points*, which is a bird with entirely different feathers.

A *net profit* deal means a percentage of the profits left over after deductions for studio overhead, fees, production costs, interest charges, marketing outlay, and a thousand other expenses. In practice, you never see a percentage of net profit because there are no net profits. The studios make money and the stars make money and the producers make money and even the investors make money. The screenwriter makes five percent of zero.

Instead of counting on the net profits of a film to provide you with your retirement fund, negotiate a deal that pays you the most U.S. currency you can possibly carry up front, that is, the highest purchase price not contingent on factors outside your control such as production dates, star commitments, or astrological convergence.

The Writers Guild Minimum Basic Agreement establishes floor rates for Guild members in all areas of television and film writing, but nothing prevents you from negotiating for a higher payment than the Guild minimum. For an original motion picture script with a budget under $2.5 million, the rate is about $45,000. For a picture costing more than $2.5 million, the fee for an original script is approximately $85,000. These amounts are adjusted upward each year that the Minimum Basic Agreement is in effect, but you can use these figures as a rough estimate of what you are likely to receive for a first-time script. Of course, you may receive considerably more if the production company desperately wants your material, in which case there is no limit to what you can ask for.

The other elements of the back-end deal are even more difficult to define than net profits. Fortunately, though, the Writers Guild MBA grants the writer some basic concessions known as *separated rights* to fix a basis for negotiation.

The MBA establishes that a Guild member who is the credited writer on original material retains the rights to publication of the material, which means

✓ the right to do a novelization

✓ the legitimate stage rights

✓ the right to be paid on the production of a sequel based on the original work

There are many areas of separated rights, however, that are less clear, and you are advised to consult a good entertainment attorney before signing any contract. Some of these areas include

✓ the rights to the characters

197

✓ the merchandising rights

✓ certain ancillary market rights, such as the emerging interactive video market

As in the case of the up-front money, nothing prohibits you from negotiating a contract that is better than the Guild MBA.

Another kind of deal that screenwriters often encounter in Hollywood is known as a *work made for hire*. A work for hire occurs when a studio or producer contracts with a writer to create a script based on an idea proposed by the writer in a pitch meeting or an idea suggested by the studio. In these cases, the studio or producer is assuming the risk by agreeing to pay the writer for his or her work even if the producer does not like the finished product.

Naturally, very few producers are going to be willing to part with their money for something they have no faith in, so most companies will offer the writer a step deal. In a step deal, the writer is engaged to produce certain limited phases in a script with payment due on completion of each stage. Generally the stages include a *treatment* or *outline*, a *first-draft screenplay*, a *second-draft screenplay*, a *rewrite*, and a *polish*. The Writers Guild sets minimums for each step and the total cannot be less than the minimum payment for a flat deal for a complete screenplay.

Of course there are as many ways to structure payments as the mind of an accountant can imagine, but two common types of payment deserve mention here. Bonus payments are promises to pay certain amounts over and above the writer's up-front fees based on specific contingencies. Commonly a writer is offered a *production bonus* if his or her version of the screenplay is actually produced as a movie *and* if the writer receives screen credit. These production bonuses can be substantial, and they are offered usually to experienced writers as an inducement to lend their talents to a project.

The other kind of back-end payment often offered to new writers is no payment at all, that is, *deferred compensation*. Particularly on very low-budget pictures produced by companies that are not signatory to the Writers Guild Minimum Basic Agreement, writers and actors and even crew members are offered deferred compensation if and when the movie makes any money. Naturally, this is a very risky proposition for the writer, but it is often the first real job a novice screenwriter receives. You will have to weigh how important immediate money is to you versus the chance to get some experience and an actual credit.

In fact, much of the deal making you will do as a screenwriter will be determined by just this consideration — do you need the money or do you need the credit? It is a question that no one can answer but you.

BREAKING INTO THE BUSINESS

So, how do you break into the business? Imagine you are standing on the platform for the bullet train. You don't know when the train will come through, and you don't know where it will go. You only know that just one window will be open. Either you jump for that window or you miss the train. Perhaps another train will come along, perhaps not. The other side of the window may drop into the restroom mop bucket, or it may open into the members-only club car. You have no way of knowing. But that window is the *only* way you have to get on the train.

Here comes the train headed your way. Are you ready to get on board? Hold on tight to your screenplay—JUMP!

SCREENWRITING 101
THE ESSENTIAL CRAFT OF FEATURE FILM WRITING

ACKNOWLEDGMENTS

My thanks to

✓ Sylvia Scott, for her expert eye and insightful heart.

✓ Pamela Karol, for her alert scholarship and thoughtful commentary.

✓ Emily Adelsohn, for her index and her devotion to the craft.

and

✓ Tracey Washington, to whom I am profoundly grateful with every word I write.

Neill D. Hicks

After doing top-secret work for an agency of the U.S. government that refuses to admit his existence, Neill naturally became a screenwriter specializing in thriller and action-adventure films and long-form television. In 1996 his work contributed to the success of the two simultaneously #1 box-office films in the world, **Rumble in the Bronx** in the U.S. and **First Strike** in Asia. Some of his other Hollywood screenwriting credits include the critically acclaimed **Dead Reckoning**, starring Cliff Robertson and Susan Blakely, as well as Pierce Brosnan's **Don't Talk to Strangers**. Recently, Neill has worked closely with European filmmakers, including the Scandinavian director Paul-Anders Simma, to create **The Minister of State** and the thriller **Ice Frontier**, currently in pre-production in Sweden. His work as a theater director includes productions as diverse as Gilbert and Sullivan's *The Mikado* and Shakespeare's *Taming of the Shrew*. Neill is a senior instructor in the UCLA Extension Writers' Program where he has been honored with the Outstanding Instructor Award; and has been a guest instructor at Northwestern University, the University of Wisconsin, the University of Denver, California State University, and the Canadian Television and Film Institute, and an advisor to the Norwegian Studiesenteret for Film, among others.

Contact Neill D. Hicks
c/o Michael Wiese Productions
11288 Ventura Blvd., Suite 821
Studio City, CA 91604
or
Point your Internet Browser to
www.screenwriting101.net

INDEX

INDEX OF FILMS CITED

THE WRITER'S JOURNEY
MYTHIC STRUCTURE FOR WRITERS - 2ND EDITION
Christopher Vogler

This new edition provides fresh insights and observations from Vogler's ongoing work with mythology's influence on stories, movies, and humankind itself.

Learn why thousands of professional writers have made THE WRITER'S JOURNEY a best-seller and why it is considered required reading by many of Hollywood's top studios! Learn how master storytellers have used mythic structure to create powerful stories that tap into the mythological core which exists in us all.

Writers of both fiction and non-fiction will discover a set of useful myth-inspired storytelling paradigms (e.g., The Hero's Journey) and step-by-step guidelines to plot and character development. Based on the work of Joseph Campbell, THE WRITER'S JOURNEY is a must for writers of all kinds.

New analyses of box office blockbusters such as Titanic, The Lion King, The Full Monty, Pulp Fiction, and Star Wars.

• A foreword describing the worldwide reaction to the first edition and the continued influence of The Hero's Journey model.

• Vogler's new observations on the adaptability of THE WRITER'S JOURNEY for international markets, and the changing profile of the audience.

• The latest observations and techniques for using the mythic model to enhance modern storytelling.

• New subject index and filmography.

• How to apply THE WRITER'S JOURNEY paradigm to your own life.

Book-of-the-Month Club Selection • Writer's Digest Book Club Selection
Movie Entertainment Book Club Selection

$22.95, 300 pages, 6 x 9
ISBN 0-941188-70-1
Order # 2598RLS

MYTH AND THE MOVIES

DISCOVERING THE MYTHIC STRUCTURE OF OVER 50 UNFORGETTABLE FILMS

NEW!

Stuart Voytilla
Foreword by Christopher Vogler, author of THE WRITER'S JOURNEY.

Ever wonder why certain movies are considered "classics" or "breakthrough films" and other films are quickly forgotten? Myth and mythic structure are often the key to defining the success factor in some of the most enduring films ever made.

Voytilla has taken the mythic structure developed by Christopher Vogler in THE WRITER'S JOURNEY and applied this idea to classic motion pictures.

MYTH AND THE MOVIES, a perfect supplement to THE WRITER'S JOURNEY, analyzes over 50 U.S. and foreign films in every cinematic genre including drama, westerns, horror, action-adventure, romance, comedy, romantic comedy, suspense-thriller, and fantasy-science fiction. This comprehensive book will give you a greater understanding of why some films continue to touch and connect with audiences, generation after generation.

Movie examples include *The Godfather, Pulp Fiction, Citizen Kane, Unforgiven, Dances with Wolves, The Silence of the Lambs, Halloween, Jaws, Raiders of the Lost Ark, The African Queen, An Officer and a Gentleman, Beauty and the Beast, The Graduate, Sleepless in Seattle, Annie Hall, Notorious, Seven, Chinatown, The Fugitive, E.T., Terminator, Star Wars,* and many more.

STUART VOYTILLA is a writer, script consultant, and teacher of acting and screenwriting.

$26.95, 300 pages, 7 x 10
ISBN 0-941188-66-3, Order # 39RLS

Available
October 1999
Advance Orders

STEALING FIRE FROM THE GODS
A DYNAMIC NEW STORY MODEL FOR WRITERS AND FILMMAKERS

James Bonnet

STEALING FIRE will take readers beyond classical story structure to an extraordinary new story model that can demonstrate how to create contemporary stories, novels, and films that are significantly more powerful, successful, and real. James Bonnet reveals the link between great stories and a treasury of wisdom hidden deep within our creative unconscious selves — a wisdom so potent it can unlock the secrets of the human mind.

Great stories are created by powerful and mysterious inner processes. The stories are designed to guide us to our full potential and are as necessary to our well-being as fresh air. Understanding great stories means understanding these inner processes can lead to a profound understanding of ourselves and the world.

This book introduces two important new models:

• The Golden Paradigm — discovery of a new psychological model brought to light by the intriguing patterns hidden within great stories.
• The Storywheel — a cosmological view of story that brings all of the different types of story together into one grand design.

Movie Entertainment Book Club Selection
JAMES BONNET, founder of Astoria Filmwrights, is a successful Hollywood screen and television writer. He has acted in or written more than 40 television shows and features including *Kojak, Barney Miller,* and two cult film classics, *The Blob,* and *The Cross and the Switchblade.*

$26.95, 300 pages, 6 x 9
ISBN 0-941188-65-5
Order # 38RLS

Available
September 1999
Advance Orders

FADE IN
THE SCREENWRITING
PROCESS - 2ND EDITION
Robert A. Berman

FADE IN is a concise, step-by-step method for developing a "story concept" into a finished screenplay.

The first edition has been used by professionals and universities around the world. The second edition covers the basics of dramatic writing; creating three-dimensional characters; screenplay structure, form, techniques, and terminology; the creative process; adaptations; and collaboration. Also included is the author's original screenplay, *Dead Man's Dance*, with agent's critique.

$24.95, 400 pages, 6 x 8-1/4
ISBN 0-941188-58-2
Order # 30RLS

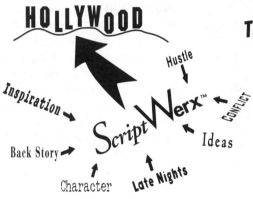

MICHAEL WIESE PRODUCTIONS
11288 Ventura Blvd., Suite 821
Studio City, CA 91604
1-818-379-8799
kenlee@earthlink.net
www.mwp.com

Write or Fax
for a
free catalog.

Please send me the following
books:

Title   Order Number (#RLS___)   Amount

_____ _____

_____ _____

_____ _____

_____ _____

SHIPPING   _____

California Tax (8.25%)   _____

TOTAL ENCLOSED _____

Please make check or money order payable to
Michael Wiese Productions

(Check one)   ___ Master Card   ___Visa   ____Amex

Credit Card Number_____

Expiration Date_____

Cardholder's Name_____

Cardholder's Signature_____

SHIP TO:

Name_____

Address_____

City_____State_____Zip_____

4/21